Jack London's Klondike Adventure

The true story of Jack London's personal odyssey from San Francisco to the Arctic Circle, across the breadth of Alaska and home again.

by

Mike Wilson

WORDSWORTH™ Sonoma County, California

ISBN# 0-9672491-0-4
Library of Congress Catalog Card Number 99-67713

First Printing – July 2001 • Limited Edition

Produced and Manufactured
in the United States of America

Cover Design and Graphics: Margie Wilson

Please note that this book was edited
from the manuscript of a forthcoming
biography on Jack London by Mike Wilson.
To contact the author or for more information on
the biography, additional copies of this book, or
information about our other Jack London products,
please contact:

WORDSWORTH™
P. O. Box 7132
Santa Rosa, CA 95407 U.S.A.
(707) 829-2316
e-mail: wwinfo@getyourwordsworth.com
http://www.getyourwordsworth.com

Table of Contents

Illustrations and Photographs

Published
in honor of
Jack London
on the
One Hundredth Anniversary
of his journey to the Klondike.

Dedication

This book is dedicated to my dear wife, Margie,
whose love and support have helped me
realize the dream of a lifetime.

Jack London circa 1897

Foreword

> "The Homer of Ninety-eight? That would be, no doubt about it, Jack London. This great master of American literature turned out the enduring stories that give most of us our introduction to Dawson and the Trail and the diggings. He, more than anyone, has immortalized that Arctic universe of gold, avarice, luck, rowdiness, heroic tragedy, low comedy."

Jack London was born on January 12, 1876, in San Francisco, California. He grew to adulthood with the specter of poverty as his constant companion. Flora, Jack's extremely self-centered mother, dominated a household that was composed of Jack, his mother, his stepfather, and two stepsisters.

Jack's stepfather, John London, had married Flora when Jack was only eight months old. John proved to be a positive and inspirational influence on his good-natured stepson.

The two stepsisters, Eliza and Ida, began living with Jack and his mother at the time of the marriage, when Eliza was twelve and Ida eight. Both girls were forbidden to reveal to Jack any hint that John London was not his natural father. This secret was successfully kept from Jack until May of 1897 when he was twenty-one years old, and John London was in his late sixties and in failing health. Though no one knows for certain how the long-kept secret was finally revealed, Jack confirmed the fact that he had been born before John London and his mother were married by looking up his own birth announcement in the newspaper archives.

This distraction occurred when Jack was in the midst of a tremendous writing effort undertaken in an attempt to earn cash to help support the family. No cash had been forthcoming, so Jack took a job at a private school in Belmont as a laundry worker. The job was outrageously demanding and paid very poorly; so, after just one month, he quit. Shortly after his return to live with his family in

Oakland, the discovery of gold in the Klondike was announced.

There have been three truly "great" gold rushes in history. All of them took place during the 19th century.

The first began on January 24, 1848, when James Marshall discovered a few flakes of gold while trying to free the wheel in the millrace of a sawmill he was building for Johann Sutter on the American River near Sacramento, California. Sutter tried to keep the discovery a secret, but the news of it was published in the *New York Herald* that August. By the end of the year, six thousand men were working in "the goldfields" of California. During the next year, 77,000 "forty-niners" would swarm to what became known as the "Golden State". Over the next seven years, the population of California grew from approximately 15,000 to almost 300,000. During that gold rush, $450 million worth of gold was found.

The second great gold rush occurred in 1851 after an Australian sheep ranch manager named Edward Hammond Hargraves found gold near Bathhurst in New South Wales. News of this discovery brought hundreds of thousands of emigrants; the population grew from 77,000 to 333,000 within one year.

The third great gold rush began on August 16, 1896, when George Washington Carmack found rich deposits of the precious metal along Rabbit Creek. This strike was on Canadian soil, in the Northwest Territories, not in Alaska as is popularly misconstrued. Two years later, because of the gold rush, this area was renamed the Yukon Territory.[1]

The discovery of gold was at the heart of a region that became known as "the Klondike" because Rabbit Creek and other creeks in that area all flowed into the larger Klondike River. About fifteen miles to the west of Rabbit Creek, the Klondike River joined the mighty Yukon River.

By 1897, $22 million worth of Klondike gold had been deposited in banks. During the next seven years, that region would yield an average of ten million dollars worth of gold annually.

All three of these great gold rushes began in what was

sparsely-settled country at the time of the initial discovery. However, once the lure of gold had attracted men and women from all walks of life, population — and with it, civilization — arrived with a vengeance. In California and Australia, many of the gold-seeking emigrants remained. But, this was not the case in the Klondike.

Unlike the gold rushes in California and Australia, the gold-seekers in the Canadian Yukon endured tremendous hardships and suffered substantial casualties. They faced rugged country, rigorous trails, and extreme weather conditions. They were also confronted with frostbite, disease, famine, and mosquitoes — not to mention the extreme difficulty of mining in frozen ground.

But the lure of gold and untold fortune made it all seem worthwhile.

Although George Carmack is given credit for beginning the Klondike Gold Rush, the finding of the first gold in the region which marked the start of the rush is not a simple story. In fact, to this day there is disagreement about who should be credited with the initial discovery. Was it Robert Henderson, the experienced prospector, who suggested that George Carmack check out Rabbit Creek? Could it have been Skookum Jim, one of Carmack's Indian companions, who was known to be an excellent prospector? Did Jim find the gold first and did Carmack dissuade him from registering the claim because he was an Indian? Or was Carmack truly the first to discover the gold?

This is a tale worth telling.

For twenty-five years, Robert Henderson had dedicated himself to the search for gold. He had panned and picked in Nova Scotia, New Zealand, Australia, and Colorado before coming to the Canadian Yukon. Henderson had been grubstaked since 1894 to prospect the Indian River as a partner of Joseph Ladue, a local trading post owner in Fortymile, the largest town in Northwestern Canada at that time. Joe Ladue had golden dreams of his own but was also a shrewd storeowner who, by hiring Henderson to search for gold, had promoted several local "strikes" that brought brisk business to his trading post.

It is important to understand that in the mid-1890s, the

area was well-populated with prospectors and miners. Several small gold rushes had already occurred in the Alaskan and Canadian regions. Also, the severe worldwide economic depression of the early 1890s had driven many men away from their homes and into the remotest regions of the world, searching for fortune and freedom from want for themselves and their families.

In his two years of searching along the Indian River, Henderson had found gold several times, though never deposits rich enough to justify his efforts and repay Ladue's expenses for his prospecting supplies. However, in the summer of 1896, while following his prospector's curiosity, Henderson climbed a round-topped mountain about ten miles northeast of the Indian River. Hiking down into a cleft on the northern side, he panned an appreciable amount of gold from the stream there on his very first try. He immediately named the stream "Gold Bottom Creek" and soon told others of the find.

While returning from a journey to pick up supplies, Henderson met George Washington Carmack at the mouth of the Klondike River. He invited Carmack to stake and work a claim at Gold Bottom.

Carmack arrived at Gold Bottom Creek with two companions and prospected near Henderson's claim but did not find enough gold to make it seem worthwhile to stay. Henderson suggested that Carmack prospect along Rabbit Creek on the other side of the ridge to their west.

As an experienced and well-known local prospector, Henderson's word carried authority; so, Carmack decided to take his advice and prospect Rabbit Creek. In exchange for Henderson's advice, Carmack agreed to send back word of any significant discovery.

At the time, Carmack was traveling with his two Indian partners, "Skookum" (which means "strong") Jim and Tagish Charley. Even though Henderson was polite to Carmack, he was intolerably rude to Carmack's Indian companions. At one point, when the Indians asked if they could buy some tobacco from him, Henderson flatly refused. This was a serious breach of backwoods etiquette. Henderson also made it clear to Carmack that he did not want any "damned Indians" staking claims on the creek.

Had Henderson known Carmack a little better, he might very well have tempered his behavior. Carmack was more than just friends with the local Indians; he lived with them and spoke their dialects fluently. Moreover, he was married to a Tagish Indian princess named Kate and was known to many as "Siwash George". Yet, even though Carmack, Tagish Charley, and Skookum Jim were deeply offended by Henderson's insults, they kept their disgust to themselves.

After leaving Henderson, the three men traveled over the ridge to the west of Gold Bottom Creek to investigate Rabbit Creek. The area had long been considered worthless "moose pasture" by local old-timers. Carmack and his companions were only casually prospecting but almost immediately found gold.

The next morning was August 17, 1896. George Carmack staked a "discovery" claim by inscribing these words on the upstream side of a blazed spruce tree:

> TO WHOM IT MAY CONCERN
> I do, this day, locate and claim, by right of discovery, five hundred feet, running up stream from this notice. Located this 17th day of August, 1896.
>
> G. W. Carmack

Carmack and his two companions went to work like demons. They panned with frying pans and otherwise improvised to remove $700,000 worth of gold dust and nuggets before leaving to record their claim.[2]

On the way to file his claim, George Carmack told every man he met of his great discovery; however, breaking a steadfast prospector's code, Carmack never sent word back to Henderson. At first, local prospectors paid little attention to Carmack's tales of a new discovery because "Lying George" had a reputation for exaggerating. But, on examining the gold Carmack carried with him, experienced sourdoughs declared that it was definitely "new gold" — gold that was unfamiliar and not recognizable as coming from a known local source. The rush began immediately.

Henderson eventually did find out about the strike when a group of men came over to Gold Bottom and told him of the finds at "Bonanza Creek". This was the name that Carmack had given Rabbit Creek shortly after making his discovery. [Bonanza means "source of wealth" in Spanish.] The name of the creek confused Henderson at first. It was only when he recognized Carmack's name that Henderson realized he had been betrayed.

Thus Robert Henderson's disdain for Indians had cost him a fortune in gold. By the time Henderson had heard of the find and traveled to Bonanza Creek, scores of local sourdoughs had already staked claims of their own.[3] Practically the entire rich strike region was claimed.[4] Within five days of Carmack's strike, the area had become a confused and frenzied scene with prospectors jumping claims, staking claims, and fighting over the outcome. It was more than six months before the anarchy would subside.

Despite the chaos, Henderson quickly staked out three claims before traveling to register them at the official Canadian government claims office where he learned that the laws pertaining to claims had recently been changed and now allowed only one claim per man. The one claim he was allowed to record was opposite Gold Bottom on Hunker Creek. Later that year when Henderson became ill, he sold the deed to this claim for three thousand dollars which he used to pay medical bills, to leave the country, and to return home to Colorado to be reunited with his wife and children.

As men began rushing to Bonanza Creek, Joe Ladue, owner of the trading post at Fortymile, recognized a tremendous business opportunity. While people scrambled madly to stake their claims along the creeks near Carmack's claim, Ladue staked out a building site on a swampy delta below Moosehide Mountain at the confluence of the Klondike and Yukon Rivers, just a few miles downstream from the strike. He registered his site, then loaded up a boat with lumber, food, and mining equipment.

Ladue soon built a warehouse which served as his new trading post. He also built a little cabin for himself which doubled as a saloon. This new two-building mining camp was the beginning of the gold-rush town of Dawson, which Ladue named after George M. Dawson, an official Canadian government geologist for the area.

Dawson (also known as "Dawson City") quickly grew into a booming gold-rush town. Along its western border flowed the mighty Yukon River, one of the longest rivers in North America. The Yukon served as a major "highway" for gold-seekers and supplies, except when it was frozen solid between November and May. Dawson became the heart of the Klondike Gold Rush and would remain the largest, most cosmopolitan town in the Northwest Territories until the summer of 1899, when 8,000 of its residents boarded paddle-wheel steamboats and rushed to a new gold strike at Cape Nome.

In a historical perspective, the Klondike Gold Rush can be best understood as occurring in several stages. The first stage involved people who were already living in the general region of the strike. Claims quickly multiplied, blanketing the area surrounding Carmack's original claim. Some of the nearby creeks actually proved to be richer in gold than Bonanza, especially one that was aptly named Eldorado.[5]

By the spring of 1897, the mining town of Dawson had grown from Ladue's two buildings into a town with 1,500 inhabitants.[6]

Early in the summer of 1897, approximately one hundred of the first miners from this gold strike left Dawson by riverboat. Many of them carried a fortune in gold that typically ranged in value from $25,000 to $500,000 per man. All of these men had worked claims along the Bonanza and its adjacent creeks. Once all of the "easy" gold had been mined, these prospectors had sold their claims and prepared to return to civilization. After months of back-breaking toil and surviving the long Arctic winter, they were more than ready to leave the Klondike and enjoy their golden riches elsewhere. Their arrival astonished the world and precipitated the second stage of the Klondike Gold Rush.

The first of these gold-laden travelers reached civilization on July 14, 1897, when the SS *Excelsior*, a seagoing passenger steamship from Alaska, arrived at the docks in San Francisco. Forty scruffy men, fresh from the Klondike, came down the gangplank carrying moosehide sacks filled with gold dust and nuggets. They went directly to the largest banks they could find to deposit their gold, and then went on a spending spree the likes of which had not been seen since the days of the forty-niners.

In a matter of minutes, rumors of a major gold strike were being whispered throughout the streets and back alleys of the city. By nightfall, the rumors had spread throughout the entire region. Urgent telegrams went out to the rest of the country. The next morning newspapers across the United States announced to the world that gold had been discovered in the Klondike.

Three days later, on July 17, the passenger steamer *Portland* docked at Seattle and unloaded sixty-eight of its own scruffy passengers also fresh from the Klondike.[7] It was reputed that this group of men brought ashore about $750,000 in gold dust and nuggets.[8] At the then-going price of $20 an ounce, this would have been 2,343 pounds total or 34.5 pounds average for each returning prospector.

With the landing of the second shipload of newly rich men from the Klondike, lightning bolts of gold strike news again shot across the country. The newspaper headlines were loud, clear calls for adventure and fortune. These calls were heard around the world by millions of souls, yearning for freedom from drudgery, want, and boredom. It seemed as though everyone was soon swept up by "Klondike Fever". Tens of thousands of men and hundreds of women from all over the world — but mostly from the United States — immediately quit their jobs, left their homes, and began the exodus northward.

It has been estimated that as many as 250,000 people left for the Klondike between 1897 and 1899. Most were waylaid, stranded, discouraged, or lost somewhere between home and the Klondike. Others were scattered throughout Alaska and Western Canada. During those three years, a total of about 50,000 travelers persevered and actually arrived at Dawson.

Among those travelers who reached the Klondike in 1897 was young Jack London, destined to become the most popular writer of his time and America's most famous Klondiker.

To twenty-one-year-old Jack London, the announcement of a huge gold strike in the Klondike meant two certain things: a chance to escape the iron grip of poverty and a clear opportunity for adventure. If he discovered gold, he would be rich and would never again do backbreaking manual labor for a menial wage. He could support his stepfather, mother, and nephew, all of whom depended on him. He would also be able to take the time to write what he pleased without concern for its commercial potential.

Writing was already London's chosen profession, but much to his disappointment, no publisher had yet offered him money for his work. However, he had been published; he had won first prize in a regional writing contest, and some of his work had been published in Oakland High School's literary magazine, *The Aegis*. In the meantime, his situation, and consequently his family's, had grown increasingly desperate.

London certainly recognized that if he traveled to the goldfields of the Klondike, a great adventure awaited him — and adventure was something he loved. He had found it as an oyster pirate at fifteen, as an able-bodied seaman at seventeen, and as a professional tramp at eighteen.

Facing the frustration of struggling to help support his family in the face of his stepfather's deteriorating health and against the prevailing hard times, Jack was more than ready for a miracle — and another adventure — when the discovery of gold was announced.

Given his background and temperament, it is scarcely surprising that Jack declared almost immediately that he would join the rush to the Klondike. In the excitement of preparing to leave, it was easy to ignore the newly revealed, dark secrets of his birth. But, it was not so easy to leave behind his ailing stepfather who begged Jack to take him along.[9]

Young Jack's quest for gold would eventually take him on a journey of more than 10,000 miles. He would witness breathtaking views, heartrending tragedy, and human triumph.

Jack London had no inkling of the changes his adventure-filled year in the Klondike would precipitate in his life.

- Mike Wilson

July 2000

Jack London in Truckee
in 1915 wearing Klondike garb

Chapter  One

Over the Chilkoot Pass

GOLD! GOLD! GOLD! GOLD!

Sixty-Eight Rich Men on the Steamer Portland.

STACKS OF YELLOW METAL!

The headlines were irresistible to Jack London, who immediately envisioned his escape from lifelong poverty. Jack had developed into a spirited and capable young man, ready to answer the call of adventure and respond to the lure of great fortune.

For Jack, the quest for gold was a quest for personal freedom. If successful, he would no longer need to work at menial jobs to finance his writing efforts. A single ounce of gold was worth the best wages he could earn in three weeks of hard, physical labor.

At the time, Jack thought that the labor he did to support his writing efforts could not possibly be any harder than looking for gold. By striking it rich in the Klondike, Jack reasoned he could "beat the system" and then do what he wanted to do . . . write.

As Jack was to recollect later, "I had to let career go hang, and was on the adventure-path again in quest of fortune".[1]

Jack knew it would cost a lot of money to go to the Klondike. Who could possibly help him finance the trip? Not his mother or stepfather who partially depended on Jack's financial assistance. Not Virginia ("Mammy Jennie") Prentiss, the nurse who had known him since birth and who had financed the purchase of his oyster-pirating ship, the *Razzle Dazzle,* when he was fifteen years old. Not Eliza Shepard, his stepsister, who had done so much to support him all his life, most recently in his efforts to gain an education.

Seeking financing for his rush to the goldfields, Jack talked to every possible person he could, but skepticism about the new gold rush was about as prevalent as optimism.

He went to see the world-famous poet, Joaquin Miller, whom Jack had recently met, only to discover that the "Sweet Singer of the Sierras" had already left for the Klondike as a reporter representing a local newspaper.[2] Using the same tactic, Jack also tried to convince a local newspaper to hire him as an exclusive reporter; but, since he lacked Miller's notoriety, all of Jack's offers were summarily rejected.

The SS *Umatilla*, a Pacific coast passenger steamship, announced it would sail for Juneau, Alaska, on Sunday, July 25th. This intensified the already rampant Klondike fever and caused an avalanche of bookings for the voyage. Jack had read the announcement of the sailing and immediately decided he wanted a ticket, but without the cash to pay for a ticket and having not found someone who would loan him the money, he began to worry about literally missing the boat.

With only four days left before the *Umatilla* was to sail, Jack unexpectedly found his financial backer — James Shepard, Eliza's husband, who was a retired Civil War Captain in his sixties.

Captain Shepard was also struck with gold fever and proposed a partnership to Jack. The conditions were that the elderly man would come along as a full partner, and Jack would pack the equipment and supplies for both of them. In exchange for Jack's labor, Captain Shepard agreed to pay for whatever supplies were needed.

Jack was ambivalent regarding Shepard's age. He was also concerned about Eliza's obvious disapproval of the entire plan. Nonetheless, Jack desperately wanted a grubstake and accepted the old soldier's terms. Eliza acquiesced to her husband's enthusiasm, and the Shepards quickly mortgaged their home to finance the imminent journey.[3]

The day after he knew he had a partner, Jack swiftly rode his bike into Oakland by way of the Lake Merritt bridge. He was to meet the Shepards downtown a little later that day. In the meantime, he had to acquire what became some of the most precious items he would take into the frozen north — books! The most important of these books proved to be Miner Bruce's Alaska, which contained the primary map and directions he would use for the entire trip.

Riding on a streetcar with Eliza on the way to meet Jack, the excitement of the moment proved too much for Captain Shepard. He suddenly collapsed in a dead faint. The driver stopped the streetcar and helped lay the unconscious old fellow out on a nearby lawn. A passerby ran for a doctor. After a quick examination, the doctor promptly prescribed two weeks of rest. James Shepard was carefully taken home and placed into bed.

When Jack heard the news about Shepard's collapse, he was devastated. When he went to see the old man the next morning, he expected the partnership proposal would be withdrawn. Instead, Shepard insisted on getting out of bed. With Jack and Eliza on each arm supporting the elderly man, the three went on a shopping spree.

Old James perked up considerably as they examined and purchased supplies. In his entire hard-pressed life, Jack had never seen such a buying binge: rugged clothes, fur caps and coats, thick mittens, long underwear, boots, tools, a tent, blankets, sled runners' rope, and thongs. The complex array of essential items they would need to survive and to prospect was purchased in a series of shops and then brought in bags and boxes to the Shepard home.

Jack already knew from newspaper reports that the Canadian government required each person coming into the Klondike to carry enough supplies to support themselves throughout the long winter months. Canadian government officials recognized that among the hordes of gold-seekers traveling over the mountain passes into the Klondike territory, many would be inexperienced in the ways of wilderness survival. The Donner Party tragedy, which had occurred only fifty years earlier, was well-remembered by these leery officials.

Understandably, many Canadians feared that famine

and other hardships which were to be expected during the long, harsh winter would also give rise to unbridled lawlessness. With this in mind, Canadian government officials enacted policies that required immigrating prospectors to carry a huge "outfit" of food, supplies, camping, and prospecting equipment. Provisions were checked by the North West Mounted Police at specially established posts inside the Canadian border and along the main routes to Dawson. Permission to continue into the Klondike could be refused to those aspiring prospectors who did not have the necessities required.

A typical outfit meeting the requirements for one man contained: 400 pounds of flour, 200 pounds of bacon, 100 pounds of beans, 100 pounds of sugar, 50 pounds of cornmeal, 50 pounds of oatmeal, 50 pounds of evaporated onions, 50 pounds of evaporated potatoes, 40 pounds of candles, 36 pounds of yeast cakes, 35 pounds of rice, 25 pounds of evaporated apples, 25 pounds of evaporated peaches, 25 pounds of evaporated apricots, 25 pounds of fish, 24 pounds of coffee, 15 pounds of salt, 15 pounds of vegetables, 10 pounds of pitted plums, 8 pounds of baking soda, 5 pounds of tea, one pound of pepper, 1/4 pound of ginger, 1/2 pound of mustard, *plus* twenty-five cans of butter, four dozen cans of condensed milk, five big bars of laundry soap, sixty boxes of matches, clothing, mosquito nets, bedding, medicine, a small steel stove, a gold pan, granite buckets, cups, plates, silverware, a frying pan, coffee pot, pick, saws, whetstones, hatchets, axes, shovels, files, a sled, ropes, pitch, oakum, *and* a canvas tent.[4] All together, a typical outfit weighed about 2,000 pounds![5]

After spending over two thousand dollars, Jack and old Captain Shepard assembled their first-class outfits in the living room of the Shepards' now-mortgaged house.[6] Once everything was carefully packed and ready to go, they said their goodbyes to family and friends.

For Jack, the hardest part of leaving was knowing that his stepfather was in very poor health. Old John London had been bedridden for weeks with a tenacious cough that taxed his one remaining lung to the limit, yet he begged Jack to take him along. The fondness he held for his stepson was evident in their poignant farewell conversations.

After leaving his stepfather's bedside, Jack lamented to Eliza, "God! — if only I could take him with me!"[7]

Most of Jack's friends wholeheartedly supported his adventure-quest in the Yukon with one notable exception — the mother of his girlfriend, Mabel Applegarth. In a revealing letter, Mrs. Applegarth clearly stated her reservations about Jack's pending departure:

> July 22nd, 1897.
>
> Dear John:
>
> We have just received your letter with the awful news that you are about to start for Alaska. Oh, dear John, do be persuaded to give up the idea for we feel certain that you are going to meet your death and we shall never see you again. What your object can be in going we cannot even think, but we feel as though we should never see you again. John, do give up the thought for you will never come back again, never. Your Father and Mother must be nearly crazed over it. Now, even at the eleventh hour, dear John, do change your mind and stay. With lots of love to all and hoping to hear better news, I remain, your sincere friend.

It is interesting to consider this communication in light of the fact that Mr. Applegarth was a mining engineer. One would think that if anyone would understand the lure of a recent gold strike, it would be a mining engineer. Perhaps the family was not in town. There is evidence that the Applegarths were in the Lake Tahoe area at this time.[8] Perhaps Mrs. Applegarth was merely expressing her personal feelings in the strongest of possible terms [although she does use the pronoun "we"].

Of course, the pleadings of Mrs. Applegarth went completely unheeded by Jack. On Sunday, July 25, three days after her letter was written, the *Umatilla* sailed north from San Francisco. It was packed with gold-seekers including young Jack London and his brother-in-law, the elderly retired American Civil War captain, James Shepard.

The ship had been scheduled to sail at nine o'clock that morning. Most of the passengers arrived at the docks in the chilly hours of dawn. The surrounding streets were mobbed with hundreds of gold-seekers and thousands of family members and friends who had come to bid them farewell. The ship was licensed to carry 290 passengers, but the

Excelsior, one of the first passenger steamers to leave San Francisco for the Klondike. July 28, 1897.
Photo by Sam C. Partridge

clamor for passage had been so intense that 471 souls were crammed into over-filled cabins and crowded onto every available foot on deck.[9]

Because of the massive traffic jam and the pandemonium at the docks, the *Umatilla* did not sail at nine. Huge mounds of outfits were piled on deck until the ship began listing to port. The captain prudently called a halt to the loading and ordered the boilers stoked. Piles of outfits and equipment were left on the dock. At ten-thirty, the big steam engines below deck were started. The excitement of the moment was apparent on every face.

At eleven o'clock, they finally set sail. From the docks came shouts of "God speed you!" A roaring, exuberant chorus responded from the ship, "Hurray for the Klondike!" The shouts and the chorus repeated again and again until the ship had sailed out of hearing range.[10] Many of those on the dock stood and watched the departing vessel until the ship was completely out of sight.

"He'll come out all right, you watch his smoke. And come out big, mark my words," John London proclaimed from his bed the day Jack sailed. The sick old man had been unable to join the crowds gathered at the docks, shouting their farewells and blessings. After Jack's departure, John was often overheard declaring to doubters, "Jack is going to make a success out of the Klondike — whether he digs it out of the grassroots or not".[11]

During the eight-day voyage northward, the primary business conducted on the ship was seeking out partners. Partners formed teams which would face the long, grueling journey to Dawson and the demands of prospecting, increasing each man's chance for success.

As part of his deal for a grubstake, Jack had already established Shepard as his first partner. He logically sought out at least two younger, more physically fit men to round out their team.

Jack did very well in his search. Soon, the young writer and his elderly traveling-mate had expanded their partnership to include three very capable men: Ira Merritt Sloper, Jim Goodman, and Fred Thompson. All three men were from Santa Rosa, California.

Merritt Sloper was a smallish, middle-aged man of forty

who only weighed about one hundred pounds, but he more than made up for his diminutive size with a wiry strength and tenacious energy. He had a cheerful, positive, yet staunch and courageous demeanor. He had just returned from South America. Sloper promised to be a valuable asset to the team with his well-developed carpentry and sailing skills, in addition to his recent experience as an adventurer.

Jim Goodman was known as "Big Jim". He brought practical mining and hunting experience to the partnership. With his impressive physical size and strength, he could easily outpack most other men.

Fred Thompson was a slender, red-whiskered young man with little outdoor experience, but his excellent physical condition together with his steady, businesslike attitude made him a good choice as a partner. He evolved into the team's organizer and recorder. His diary would become the primary resource for all who would later study Jack London's trek into the Yukon.

The steamship took the gold-hungry throng north to Port Townsend where many of the passengers (including Jack, James Shepard, and their three new-found partners) transferred to another passenger steamship, the *City of Topeka*. They sailed on this ship to Juneau, Alaska, arriving on the second of August. They spent three days in Juneau on a stopover and arranged for passage further north.

On August fifth, at eleven o'clock in the morning, they left Juneau traveling in impressive seventy-foot Indian canoes which had been made from single, hollowed-out tree trunks. For the next two days, they were paddled northward, through the gargantuan beauty of the Inside Passage. They traveled past Auke Bay, then along the shoreline of Favorite Channel. Next, they entered the great Lynn Canal which on the maps pointed north like a finger of blue towards the rugged Klondike.

They camped each night on rocky beaches. Finally, after riding in the big canoes for about one hundred miles, they were paddled up the Taiya Inlet and came to a place known as Dyea ["Ty-A"].

Jack and his group arrived at Dyea at three-thirty in the afternoon on August 7, 1897.[12] This small settlement stood on the northernmost edge of Lynn Canal and the Inside

Passage.

It was fortunate for Jack and his partners that they had taken native canoes which could float over the shallow water approaching the shore and land on the beach at Dyea. The scene that prevailed there was a picture of gold rush madness. Offshore, an odd assemblage of ships was anchored where the water was still deep enough to insure that they would not be grounded by surprise. Rowboats, flatboats, canoes, and rafts were used to ferry people, supplies, and equipment the remaining distance to shore. Frantic men worked desperately hard to land mobs of people and mountains of goods. Horses and many other animals were usually forced to swim.

In A Daughter of the Snows, published five years later, Jack dramatized what he witnessed at Dyea: "Everybody was in everybody else's way; nor was there one who failed to proclaim it at the top of his lungs. A thousand gold-seekers were clamouring for the immediate landing of their outfits. Each hatchway gaped wide open, and from the lower depths shrieking donkey-engines were hurrying the misassorted outfits skyward. On either side of the steamer, rows of scows received the flying cargo, and on each of these scows a sweating mob of men charged the descending slings and heaved bales and boxes about in frantic search. Men waved shipping receipts and shouted over the steamer-rails to them. Sometimes two and three identified the same article, and war arose".[13]

The intensity of the unloading frenzy was synchronized with a devastating thirty-foot tide. Twice a day, a series of small "tidal waves" came rushing in toward the shore. One of these waves could easily capsize and wreck a small boat or raft — and often did — with tragic and heartbreaking results. Being caught by the incoming tide could quickly destroy a gold-seeker's dreams. Imprudent men would drown trying to save lost equipment in the frigid, bone-chilling waters.

Some of the gold-seekers arriving as the ebb tide began were foolishly casual. The outgoing tide moved astonishingly fast, revealing the silt-and-sand bottom of the bay which seemed to suddenly emerge. Boats filled with men and equipment could be unexpectedly grounded hard and fast.

This outgoing flood was also very capable of drowning or injuring a man. In the quickly receding tide, valuable supplies and equipment could easily be washed away or destroyed.

Once the tide turned back toward the shore, men worked with an increasing urgency to move their beached belongings out of the reach of the charging tidal waves and above the high tide line. Confusion reigned. Tempers flared as men grew increasingly desperate and struggled to beat the onrushing water. This madness would reach its crescendo as the final waves of the high tide rushed in and lapped at the high water mark. In the frenzy to unload men and equipment, many fights broke out. Disputes were often settled violently with fists, knives, clubs, pick axes, shovels, or guns.

No accurate account was kept of the injured, wounded, or dead.

It was clear to Jack and his partners that they should get away from the madness as quickly as they could. After wrestling their outfits to above the high water mark, they purchased a rowboat for ten dollars. Guiding the small craft with ropes from the shore, they began to ferry their outfits away from the beach.

They pulled the boat up the Taiya (Dyea) River which flowed into the apex of the inlet from a steep-sided mountain valley. This lush valley was about two-thirds of a mile across near the mouth of the river but quickly narrowed into a canyon as it reached inland. Above the valley, the coastal mountains stood like a huge, five thousand foot wall between Dyea and the Klondike.

Fifteen miles to the north, the impressive Chilkoot Pass formed a saddle between two majestic peaks. The pass was thirty-five hundred feet above where they stood on the beach. The path Jack and his partners were taking to the Pass would eventually be known by gold rush travelers as "the meanest thirty-two miles in history"[14] and "the worst trail this side of hell".[15] [Today "the world's longest museum" is considered by many to be "the most beautiful 32 miles in Alaska and British Columbia".[16]]

On the second day, August 8, the weather was clear and warm. Jack wrote a letter to Mabel Applegarth. Here are a few excerpts:

> I am laying on the grass in sight of a score of glaciers, yet the slight exertion of writing causes me to sweat prodigiously.
>
> We lay several days in Juneau, then hired canoes & paddled 100 miles to our present quarters. The Indians with us brought along their Squaws, papooses & dogs. Had a pleasant time. The 100 miles lay between mountains which formed a Yosemite Valley the whole length, & in many places the heights were stupendous. Glaciers and waterfalls on every side. Yesterday a snow slide occurred & the rumble & roar extended for fully a minute. . . .
>
> Am certain we will reach the lake in 30 days.
>
> Including Indians there are about 2000 people here & half as many at Skagawa Bay [Skagway], 5 miles from here.[17]

The many trails leading inland from the long beach converged into a wide dirt path that led due north away from the shoreline and followed the east bank of the Taiya River through the ramshackle town of Dyea, less than a mile away. Because their boat was small and their outfits were large, many trips back and forth were required to move their belongings upstream. After pulling their repeated boatloads upriver and through the town, Jack and his partners entered a lush coastal rain forest. Poplars, interspersed with elder, willow, and birch trees thickly lined the shores of the river, obscuring the mountainsides around them.

As they traveled upriver, they had to cross several tributary streams, splashing or wading across these streams as they towed their boats with ropes from the shore. This led to cold, wet feet and was only a sample of what was to come.

About five miles upstream from the mouth of the river, roaring cascades above them signaled the end of boat navigation. From the bottom of these first falls, the outfits would have to be packed.

Along the riverbank and on the trail that ran parallel to it, swarms of voracious mosquitoes surrounded each man like a cloud of misery, following him everywhere he went. Men covered their skins with obnoxious ointments and smoked tobacco like fiends to dissuade the hungry insects as much as they possibly could. Most simply suffered along, absent-mindedly fanning the pests away from their faces. Some men went mad with the buzzing little predators, and more than one man is said to have taken his life *just to escape the mosquitoes!*

The trailhead staging area at the cascades was referred to as "the Flats" and was later known as Canyon City.[18] Jack and his partners sold their boat and prepared to hike. Unseen through the dense foliage, snow-laden mountains rimmed with blue-ice glaciers towered majestically on three sides above them, most often shrouded in mist and clouds. From the crowded and cluttered beach behind them to the rocky heights before them, an unbroken, ant-like column of men slowly ascended the Chilkoot Trail.

The ranks of the struggling gold-seekers were swollen by hundreds of Indian packers — men, women and children. Most of these packers were from the local coastal tribe of Chilkats, closely related to the Siwash Indians. There were also members of the nearby Tlingit, Stick, and Tagish tribes.

Some available Indian packers met new arrivals on the beach, but the favorite spot for hiring packers was in front of Healy's trading post in the town of Dyea where there were scales for weighing packs. Packers were also frequently hired in the adjacent Indian village. Meeting descending, unemployed packers while ascending the trail was the last chance to hire a packer.[19]

In the early spring of 1897, the fee for an Indian packer had been only eight cents a pound.[20] By August, when Jack and his partners arrived, the rate had increased to thirty cents[21] and was sometimes as high as fifty cents[22] per pound. This meant it would cost an arriving gold-seeker from three to five hundred dollars to have his one-thousand-pound outfit carried up to the summit. To complicate matters, the Indians and other packers would only accept gold or silver coins since they had been swindled with counterfeit paper money earlier in the year.

This unexpected expense stopped many would-be Klondikers cold. The majority initially declared they would pack their own outfit. They soon realized what this entailed. Since no one could possibly pack all of their supplies and equipment in one trip up to the pass, those choosing to carry their outfits themselves were forced to pack portions of it in a series of heavy loads, usually from 75 to 100 pounds each. Under the weight of a 100-pound load, an inexperienced packer found it difficult to stand up and stay on his feet, let alone trudge uphill on the rugged trail. Only strong, experienced packers (like Jack) were capable of performing the task for themselves. The stronger, more experienced Indian packers could carry as much as 160 pounds at a time.

Many new arrivals who tried to carry their own outfits gave up within the short stretch of trail between the shoreline and town. If a Klondiker could not pack his own outfit, he must agree to pay whatever the Indian packers asked. If he did not have the money to pay packers, he would be forced to abandon the journey, seeking passage out on the next available boat.

Jack's partner, Fred Thompson, reportedly paid a bargain rate of 22 cents per pound [a total of $660] to have his 3,000-pound outfit carried to the summit of Chilkoot Pass.[23] Although most of the new arrivals somehow managed to pay the portage, Dyea soon grew crowded with men who had been ill-prepared and now found themselves stymied.

Jack London and Captain Shepard could not afford to pay the packers. However, by the terms of their agreement, Jack was responsible for packing both his own and the old man's outfits.

On August 12, Jack and his partners took their places in the line of packers and followed the column moving upward like ants.[24] The outfits were hiked one pack-load at a time up a segment of trail the length of which was determined by the trail's difficulty, the size of the outfits, and the number of packers. Generally, a partner stayed with the forward pile, another partner remained with the base cache, while the others trekked in-between. On reaching the forward pile, a packer would remove and unload his pack. After resting, he would return downhill for another load. This routine, which grew out of the necessity of moving the heavy outfits, also discouraged stealing by others on the trail.

Through trial and error, Jack discovered he could carry seventy-five to one hundred pounds at a time. Yet, even with one hundred pound loads, he traveled thirty-nine miles — twenty of these miles carrying his pack uphill — for every mile a complete outfit was advanced up the trail. This was why Jack explained to Mabel in his August 8th letter that it would take thirty days to pack the thirty-two miles to the lakes on the other side of Chilkoot Pass.

As the canyon began to narrow, the river became a series of cascades and the climbing began in earnest. For the next eight miles, they trudged and grunted uphill as part of the packers' line. On return trips for another load, they would scramble over boulders and logs down the sides of the trail so as not to impede those struggling upward.

At first, they hiked through a forest of tough, weather-beaten evergreens surrounded by moss-slick boulders. As they progressed, there was more fallen timber, more boulders, and many piles of rock. Following the meandering trail, they crossed tributary streams and the roaring river many times — wading in ice-cold waters, jumping from rock to rock, and straining for tenuous balance over hastily-made footbridges.

Captain Shepard had been designated as the group's cook. However, because of his age and physical condition, he was not much help packing the outfits, although he did what he could. Even without much to carry, the old man became exhausted just climbing the trail to where the cascades began. Jack uncomplainingly took up the slack for his elderly partner, but his shoulders were soon raw and terribly sore from packing the brunt of their two outfits.

By August 14, they had ascended to a sparsely-forested region of loose moraine which was characterized by big piles of smooth rocks and sand deposited by ancient glaciers.

The weather was decidedly hot. Jack stripped down to his long, red flannel underwear, bringing blushes and guffaws from others on the trail.[25] To lessen the number of trips under these conditions, he carried as much as one hundred and fifty pounds at a time. Jack's partners were concerned by his extraordinary exertion.

Finally, old Captain Shepard, complaining of rheumatism, wisely decided to return home to Oakland. It was one of the happiest moments of Jack's life because he no longer had to pack two outfits.[26]

The two original partners said an amiable farewell.

Shepard left most of his outfit for Jack to dispose of as best he could and departed down the trail towards the beach to catch the next available boat going south.

The next day, Fred Thompson accepted the duties of cook, which had been Shepard's job. That same day, a new man joined Jack and his remaining partners; this was Martin W. Tarwater from Santa Rosa, California. Jack later immortalized Tarwater in "Like Argus of the Ancient Times".[27]

According to Thompson's diary, Tarwater was not a partner but a "passenger exchanging board and passage for his work".[28] However, in time he proved to be an important addition to the team by helping with cooking, packing, and repairing shoes.

Tarwater was concerned about being allowed into the Klondike because he did not have all the materials in his outfit that were required by the Canadian government.[29] It is likely that Jack traded part of Shepard's outfit to Tarwater, but this may not have been necessary since the trail was becoming littered with discarded belongings left by those who had already abandoned the quest or who had simply discovered they had more than they needed.

The next few days were very hard. Along with hundreds of others on the trail, Jack and his partners continued their struggle to the summit.

Seldom in history have so many willingly suffered so much for so little. Men would fall under the weight of heavy packs then grimly rise again or finally give up the whole idea and cry in defeat and despair. The sound of a single gunshot often signaled the tragic end of a would-be gold-seeker who was too tired to continue and too embarrassed or proud to go back. Such was the lot of men who allowed their hearts to be broken while ascending the Chilkoot Trail. Others accepted the suffering bravely, offering help wherever they could, giving a kind or encouraging word to those in the deepest despair.

A "down" trail did not exist for those who chose to return rather than continue their ascent. Because the established path was filled with those climbing, any descent was made to the sides. This scrambling downward over untrampled mountain terrain could be very dangerous since a man could easily slip, trip, or fall in the mud or on the mossy, often rain-wet rocks and logs.

Many men on the trail were injured. Most mishaps were minor and those injured could continue. A more serious injury could mean death unless the hurt man could return down the trail and find medical attention or quick transportation to Juneau.

Some men were not that lucky and died from their injuries sustained on the trail. Those whose bodies were not returned home were often buried in a make-shift cemetery outside of the town of Dyea. Many were buried near the trail. Within a few years, most poorly-marked trailside graves were indistinguishable from the rugged landscape.

Pack animals suffered worse than men and were normally forced to carry their absolute limit. Horses, mules, and donkeys constituted the majority of pack animals, but even dogs and goats were used to help transport outfits uphill.

Many animals were simply abused, not properly cared for or fed. As a result, numerous animals died on the trail, often at the hands of gold-blind, insane men feverish to gain the summit of Chilkoot and caught up in a frenzy of disgust and despair. Others drowned during the repeated crossings of the roaring river's icy waters whose bed the trail generally followed.

Jack London had always loved animals. The sickening trailside spectacle created by piles of dead animals, mostly horses, was a sight he would never forget.[30]

Jack's adventure expanded to the dimensions of the colossal landscape. As he frequently had in the past, Jack quickly learned and adapted to the lessons and hardships of the situation. On his journey, he saw both heroism and tragedy unfold before him. He was inspired by acts of kindness and courtesy but was also disgusted by greed-driven selfishness. Jack could see that men either rose in stature to match the challenges of the Klondike or were reduced to victims of its might. In his writer's soul, London felt an immense inspiration in the raw, wild beauty of it all.

At one point, while plodding painfully upward, Jack happened to glance to the side of the trail and noticed a pair of snow-crusted boot soles barely protruding from behind a large trailside log. His curiosity aroused, Jack carefully turned out of line and went to the log to investigate. He discovered a man trapped upside down by the weight and straps of the pack on his back. The man had toppled backwards while resting on the log, and none of the other packers — focused intently on the trail at their feet — had noticed the fellow go over. Jack removed his own pack and helped the sputtering, red-faced man out of his dangerous predicament. The man declared that he had been afraid for his life and expressed profuse gratitude. London replaced his own pack and continued up the trail.[31]

Jack and his partners trudged on. Everyone's feet became terribly sore as the trail grew extremely rugged. The stretch of trail they tackled on August 17 was so difficult that they made only three-quarters of a mile headway for the entire day.[32]

The next day the sky was overcast. A drizzle began with nightfall, and they awoke the following morning to rain. Now, they faced a muddy trail that at times became a stream. Ascending the slippery trail in the cold rain was miserable.

As the weather continued to cool, the rain fell unremittingly. Their clothes became soaked through to the skin. Men tried to keep warm by packing as hard as they could; but, when they needed to rest, a chill would set in very quickly. Fires were of utmost importance to the soaked and shivering men, but fires had become very difficult to build with the sparse trailside wood being wet.

Ten miles up the trail from the beach where they had landed, there was a relatively level and open series of meadows designated by a trailside sign as "Pleasant Valley".[33] The sign seemed a little sarcastic to Jack and his partners as they slogged — wet, cold, and foot-sore — through the area in the pouring rain.

It was August the twentieth, and their effort to make progress was anything but pleasant. As they searched for a good spot to camp, they discovered that the water-saturated soil of the meadow had been transformed into a sea of deep, cold mud by the hundreds of men tramping through it during two days of steady rains. "Pleasant Valley" (more commonly known later as "Pleasant Camp") was a combination of impromptu gold rush campground and mud bog.

Despite the inclement weather, the next day of packing was very successful. They progressed over three miles of trail, including three river crossings.

The next stop they made was at a place called Sheep Camp. Here, they found large outcroppings of rock, massive piles of boulders, and a veritable jumble of pine, spruce, and fir trees. At least there was plenty of fuel and many places to build a sheltered fire, slightly out of the rain. It would have been a good place to stay for the night, but instead they decided to press on to try to reach the next landmark on the trail, Stone House, a huge boulder shaped like a house.[34]

But, the rocky rubble of the mountainside they were ascending made the going extremely hard. By the afternoon of August 22, they had only progressed a short way above Sheep Camp. It was Sunday, and the weather had cleared and warmed. Jack and his partners were exhausted, so they spent the afternoon snoozing while Tarwater repaired their tattered shoes and boots.[35] Above them, through the tall, stark trunks of the trees on the ever-thinning edge of the coastal forest, they could see the imposing peaks that formed the summit.

At dawn the next day, the rain resumed. After eating breakfast, they set out again. The landscape dictated the length of each segment of trail they tackled. As they approached the summit, the increasingly steep and rugged trail required the segments to be shortened.

It continued to rain as they crossed the timberline. The trail grew steeper and even more rugged. It led to the upper escarpment of the mountain which looked as if it went straight up and, at times, gave the impression of leaning directly overhead. With tremendous effort they hefted their packs and plodded on in the rain with stoic, unspoken exhaustion.

Once above the timberline, they found themselves in a woodless, glacier world where fires were few and precious. It took much more effort to gather firewood on this upper section of the Chilkoot Pass Trail. In fact, they usually had to travel far down the trail, to below the timberline, to find enough wood to build an effective fire.

Most men were just too tired to make the extra round trips for wood. Instead, they would shiver and try to rest while burrowed into a pile of their gear in the hollow of a boulder or under the overhanging edge of a blue-iced glacier.

Progressing up the trail they entered a gigantic gorge that led to the final ascent. This stretch of gorge was the most dangerous part of the trail. In fact, only two weeks after Jack and his partners passed through this area, a landslide came crashing down the mountain wiping out a large section of the trail. At least one man was killed and several others were injured. Tents and outfits were smashed and buried under tons of mud, rock, and ice.[36]

The last two miles of the ascent were obstructed by boulders and rocks of all sizes. The ground was also littered with broken and sharp-edged shale, making footing unstable.[37] The knife-like stones soon cut apart tattered footwear.

Progress up the trail was slow. They clawed, wrestled, and balanced their way over countless rocks of every size including huge boulders and jagged outcroppings.

The trail crossed the ice-cold river headwaters again and again, switching sides to follow the best route upward. They crossed precarious log footbridges, fully aware that a hapless slip could lead to a horrible death — bludgeoned by a fall onto rocks below or drowned in the river by the weight of a pack.

This last stretch of the trail to the summit was steep. It was more like a narrow, precipitous staircase than a trail.

Horses, mules, and donkeys could no longer be forced to climb. Besides, there was no forage growing for miles after crossing the summit. An animal would have had to been loaded to its capacity just to pack its own food. Continuing to use these pack animals would have been foolish and impractical. So, at this point on the trail, packs were removed from the horses, mules, and donkeys.

This reprieve from the weight of the loads preceded a moment of life-or-death judgment for each animal. If an owner considered an animal to still be in useful condition, it would be sold and taken back to the beach to repeat the long haul up the trail. However, if an animal was in poor condition, its fate would not be pleasant. The fact was that most of the animals on the trail were not properly cared for and deteriorated quickly. Horseshoes and nails were in short supply; veterinarians and blacksmiths were preoccupied with the gold rush. Tragically, the majority of animals were simply used and discarded.

Horses, mules, and donkeys judged to be unfit were killed or abandoned on this section of the trail. The bodies of hundreds of pack animals were often piled in huge "holes", natural depressions beside the trail. Sometimes these animals were still alive, wallowing helplessly until they eventually died. Men often grew disgusted with this ghastly spectacle and shot the animals to end their suffering.

Other pack animals were simply unloaded and left to wander aimlessly along the trail. These poor, bewildered creatures would drift away from the trail until they were forever lost in the gigantic landscape.

Dogs and goats were usually taken over the summit but faced life-threatening hardships while traversing the hundreds of miles to Dawson.

On the twenty-fourth of August, it rained all day. Conditions on the trail were abysmal. After making three round trips, Jack and his partners stayed in camp for the rest of the day, hoping the weather would clear. With nightfall, they hoped the rain would abate before daybreak. They settled in for a cold, wet night.

The rain continued throughout the night. In the morning, they became concerned that the pass could be closed by a snowstorm if the weather grew colder. If it snowed, they would be forced to descend to below the timberline and wait for the weather to clear. If the weather did not sufficiently clear, they could feasibly be stuck in the Dyea Valley until winter and might be forced to abandon their quest.

With this unsavory prospect in mind, the five men decided to push on, regardless of the constant rain. Their perseverance was rewarded. By the end of the day, they pitched camp at Stone House.

That evening the rain poured down on Jack and his partners as they hunkered around a small fire near Stone House and wished for a break in the weather, but the rain continued throughout the night.

On the morning of the twenty-fifth, the weather seemed worse . . . but the summit was less than a mile ahead! In spite of the unrelenting rain, Jack and his partners decided to continue.

Some Klondike gold-seekers trying the route through Dyea gave up their quest on this final stretch of the trail, but not Jack London, Jim Goodman, Fred Thompson, Merritt Sloper, or old Mr. Tarwater. Nose-to-heel they climbed together, jammed into the line of other packers, ascending on steps created by the feet of men who had climbed this path before them. They were burning with an almost vengeful determination to conquer the Chilkoot Pass, but the way was made hard by the cold, wind-blown rain, the weight of the packs on their backs, and the straps that cut into their shoulders.

The rain did not stop nor did it get much worse; so, Jack and his partners continued. They plodded on, one step up at a time, one foot in front of the other. With the rain still coming down, Jack and his partners reached the last flat piece of ground before Chilkoot Pass called "The Scales". Surrounded on three sides by steep mountain slopes, this narrow boulder and shale-strewn terrace was no bigger than several football fields and lay at the base of the grey wall of rock that was the last and most imposing obstacle just before the summit.[38] Klondikers reweighed their supplies here, and the packers' rates per pound increased before the final ascent.

Thompson noted in his diary:

> We camped on the cold rocks with ice-cold water running underneath then gathered what brush and moss we could find spread it on our rocky floor in [the] tent, ate our scanty supper and we had barely wood enough to get breakfast with as we had to pack it 2 miles, spread our blankets and tried to get some sleep laying on the soft side of many sharp stones.[39]

Chilkoot Pass lay directly ahead at the top of a craggy cliff. There were two main routes up to the Pass. One was a long, winding, narrow ravine trail used mostly by those with dog teams or livestock. The second and most frequently used route was about three-fourths of a mile in length and lay through a jumble of boulders at the bottom of the cliff. This route then broke into a half-dozen smaller trails that zigzagged up and over a series of ledges that composed its face. The path was deceptively steep in appearance when seen from below, yet its slope averaged only 45°.

The final 150-foot segment of trail before attaining the Pass included a series of crudely-hewn steps known to optimistic Klondikers as "the Golden Stairs".

On Friday, August 28, Jack and his partners began making trips to the summit. Faced with a steady deluge and gale-force winds, they were surprised to discover the final assault was easier than they had expected. Still, it should be remembered that this short distance would be magnified by the ten to fifteen pack-loads required to move a complete outfit to the top of the trail.

At last, on August 30, they stood 3,600 feet above the beach at Dyea with their outfits piled beside them in the saddle of Chilkoot Pass.

The worst part of getting their outfits to this lofty elevation was the miserable weather they found there. Had the weather been clear, they certainly would have enjoyed a breathtaking view. As it was, the weather was awful. Chances are they saw very little from the summit of the trail. Rain fell from rolling clouds above them and a swirling mist blew all around them.

The inclement weather and the approach of nightfall forced them to camp overnight on the barren rocks. The camp was very uncomfortable. Everyone in Jack's party was drenched and thoroughly chilled by the wind-driven rain. This description from Jack's later fiction draws on his memories of Chilkoot Pass:

> . . . Wet to the waist, famished and exhausted, he would have given a year's income for a fire and a cup of coffee. Instead, he ate half a dozen cold flapjacks and crawled into the folds of a partly unrolled tent. . . .
>
> In the morning, stiff from his labors and numb with the frost, he rolled out of the canvas, ate a couple of pounds of uncooked bacon, buckled the straps on a hundred pounds, and went down the rocky way.[40]

The Chilkoot Pass Summit, Summer 1897,
the same summer Jack London traversed it.

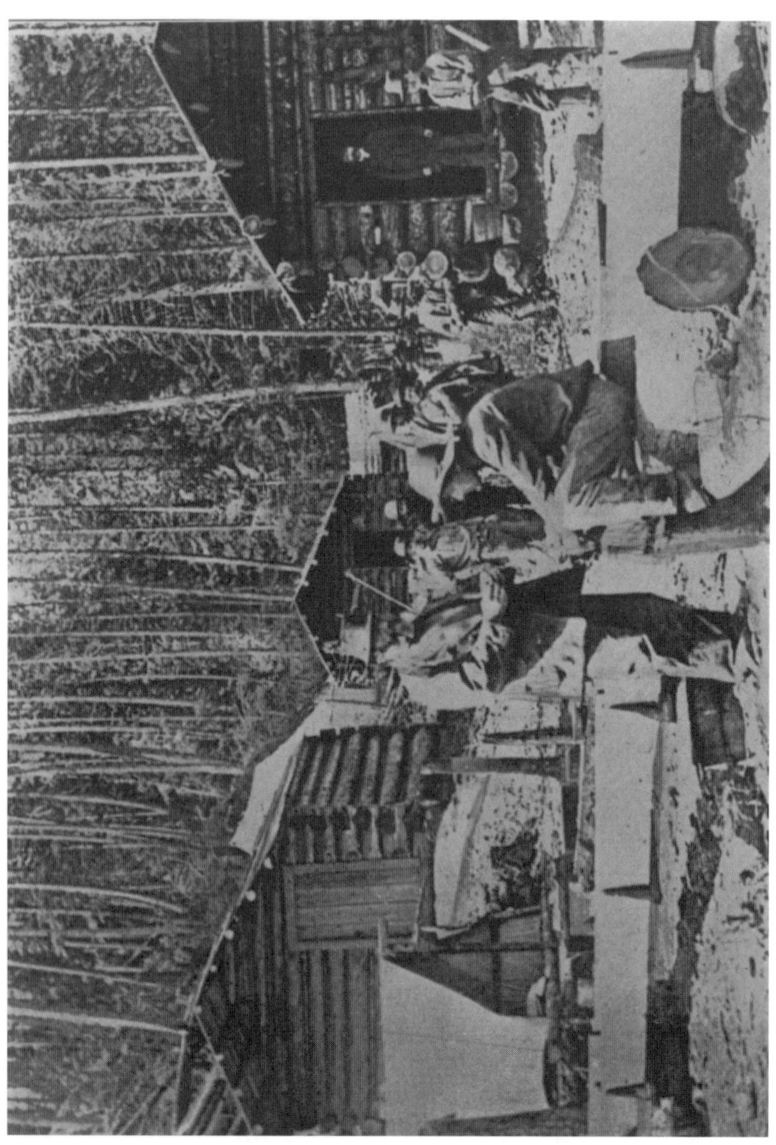

Klondikers and miners' cabins in Dawson City
during the early days of the gold rush.

CHAPTER TWO

Life and Death in the Klondike

For those who conquered the Chilkoot Pass, the struggle to reach the goldfields was just beginning. They now started the second leg of their race to file a claim: transporting themselves and their outfits the remaining 600 miles to Dawson City (more commonly known as Dawson) at the heart of this Klondike Gold Rush. They would still need to find gold on unclaimed ground, stake it out, and file a claim.

Untrained or misinformed about prospecting, many *cheechakos* [the Klondike term for "greenhorn"] never found gold. For those whose prospecting techniques or knowledge of geology led to the discovery of gold, the official government office in Dawson would accept and acknowledge their claim.

The race against the life-threatening onslaught of winter had to be faced by everyone in the Klondike, including the newly-arriving *cheechakos*. If winter caught them unprepared, they could easily perish. It was essential to find or build a cabin for shelter, gather ample firewood, and stock in supplies before the snows began. Many of those who failed to make themselves ready, especially many newcomers, faced severe consequences or death.

Once they had conquered the Chilkoot Pass, Jack and his companions began a new type of trail aptly described as "a series of flats, mountains, hills, water, mud, quagmires and bogs from one end to the other".[1]

Luckily for his partners, Jack was an extraordinarily adept, improvisational camper. The skills he had learned as a tramp would help them all on the trail to the goldfields. In later years, Fred Thompson commented that Jack London was such an "expert at out-of-doors life" that "he could kindle a fire in a storm, make delicious flapjacks and bacon, sling a tent so they could sleep warmly in a temperature of thirty degrees below zero".[2]

On the morning of August 31, 1897, the first thing that Jack and his companions did was to move their outfits down the other side of the pass. They crossed a snowfield over a small glacier, then packed down the two miles of trail to the southern shore of Crater Lake. It was amazing how comparatively quick and easy it was to move their outfits downhill.

Along the shore, they found themselves in a growing bustle of men. They quickly hired a boat to transport them the three miles across the lake to the northern shore.

The group was in good spirits as they camped that night on the north shore of Crater Lake. They had made very good progress.

One of the rewards of life in the higher latitudes is the breathtaking phenomenon of the aurora borealis. Gargantuan, vertical curtains of iridescent luminescence appear regularly in the nocturnal skies of the Arctic adding a surreal touch to the already daunting aspects of climate and geography.

Jack and his partners first saw these displays in the northernmost nighttime skies as they canoed toward Dyea. While ascending the Chilkoot Pass, their view of the northern skies was obscured by the range of coastal mountains they were climbing. However, once they reached the Pass and the north side of the mountains, they could observe and enjoy not only a panoramic view, but also the aurora borealis.

At times in his future literature, Jack would write of these northern lights. In A Daughter of the Snows, Jack described this "flaming triumph":

> Suddenly, like the ray of a search-light, a band of white light ploughed overhead. Night turned to ghostly day on the instant, then blacker night descended. But to the south-east a noiseless commotion was apparent. The glowing greenish gauze was in a ferment, bubbling, uprearing, downfalling, and tentatively thrusting huge bodiless hands into the upper ether. Once more a cyclopean rocket twisted its fiery way across the sky, from horizon to zenith, and on, and on, in tremendous flight, to horizon again. But the span could not hold, and in its wake the

> black night brooded. And yet again, broader, stronger, deeper, lavishly spilling streamers to right and left, it flaunted the midmost zenith with its gorgeous flare, and passed on and down to the further edge of the world. Heaven was bridged at last, and the bridge endured![3]

The next morning was the first of September. The weather was still wet and cold, but the five men were determined to get through the Pass. They rose early, ate breakfast, shouldered their packs to continue downhill, and started their assault on the interior of the Klondike with a series of short, forced marches.

Jack and his party were obviously in good physical condition since they made the initial trek from Crater Lake down the Dyea Trail to Happy Camp, just south of Long Lake, in a single day. It was only four miles between the two lakes, but the trail was as rugged as ever, and they still had to make many repeated trips to transfer an entire outfit, one pack at a time. The complete transfer of their outfits to Happy Camp took Jack's group five days.

Traveling along the trail with them were hundreds of others. Most were doggedly trudging downhill with packs or vigorously returning uphill for more. For men already exhausted from the long climb up to the Pass, even the downhill hike was too much. As Jack would later write, "Men broke their hearts and backs and wept beside the trail . . . But winter never faultered".[4]

On September 6, Jack and his companions paid thirty dollars to be ferried with their outfits by boat across the aptly-named Long Lake. This was the first in a series of small glacial lakes which eventually drained into the headwaters of the mighty Yukon River.[5] Once they had reached the headwaters, their path would become a swift-moving highway of water all the way to the goldfields.

From the northern shore of Long Lake, Jack's party packed the approximately three hundred yards down the trail to the southern edge of the next lake, known as "Deep Lake".

On the seventh, they finished piling their outfits on the south shore of Deep Lake. They arranged to be ferried the less than one-half mile length of this small lake for a fee of eight dollars.

A cascading stream roars out of Deep Lake to the next mountain lake, Lake Lindeman (also spelled by many as "Linderman"). This stream descends more than one thousand feet in less than a mile and a half and includes many spectacular rapids and waterfalls. Navigation down the stream was therefore not feasible, so the partners hiked down the steep, narrow canyon that led to Lake Lindeman. They arrived at this lake on the exact date Jack had predicted in his August eighth letter to Mabel Applegarth.

They bivouacked the next day on the south shore of Lake Lindeman, which was the beginning of their small boat navigation into the Klondike. This was important since they would use the lakes and rivers to travel north to Dawson. Lake Lindeman marked the end of the Chilkoot Trail, which was considered the best — the most established, most direct, safest, and fastest — route to the Yukon.

About one hundred and fifty other tents were pitched along the southern shore of the lake near their camp. Half a dozen sawpits were in constant use as singing, confident men sawed logs from nearby spruce trees into rough, unfinished boards. These boards were used to construct from six to ten boats a day which were regularly launched amid celebratory cheers and pistol shots.[6]

On September ninth, Merritt Sloper and Jack London joined William Odette, Dave Sullivan, and someone known only as "Jud". These five men represented two partnerships combining their efforts to build two boats, one for each party.

Because practically all of the usable lumber surrounding the lakeshore had already been cut, the team of five men hiked five miles up a tributary river before finding a good stand of trees.[7] Once they had set up a camp, the men began to work feverishly. They toiled unrelentingly from sunup until long after dark. At the end of each day, unable to work anymore, they returned to their tents and collapsed in utter exhaustion.

Fred Thompson made a daily, five-mile hike up from the base camp on the shore of Lake Lindeman to the five-man team's boat-building camp. Throughout each day, he served as cook, fixing meals for the hard-working team.

From the pervasive, mostly-spruce forest, they cut trees into logs using axes, hatchets, and saws. The logs were then placed over a saw-pit, and using what Jack would later deem as "an inadequate whipsaw", they cut enough raw lumber to build two boats.

How were five men with only packable hand tools able to build two rough-hewn but nonetheless sturdy, seaworthy boats in ten days? The "secret" was that living and surviving was difficult in the 1890s. Long hours and hard work were common. People did what was necessary or suffered the consequences of failure.

The boats would be used to travel the remaining 600 miles of waterways from Lake Lindeman to Dawson. Both of the newly-built boats were considered top-notch, a testament to the team of novice shipbuilders and Sloper's boat-building experience. One craft was christened the *Yukon Belle* and the other, the *Belle of the Yukon*. These names serve as good examples of the wry humor shared by Klondikers.

The boats were "lined" (controlled by rope tethers from shore) downstream for about two miles. The swift-flowing mountain river with its cascading falls, rapids, and rocks made this a very ticklish job. One slip of a rope could easily result in the total destruction of a boat. But, after two miles of lining, the water's increasing depth made it more practical to take the boats for a "very lively ride down the swift and crooked river".[8]

Once they had reached the lake, the boats were divided between the two parties. Jack's party, which included Goodman, Sloper, Thompson, and Tarwater, would sail in the *Yukon Belle*. The crew of the *Belle of the Yukon* was made up of Odette, Sullivan, Jud (from the boat-building crew), Charles Rand, and a Mrs. Hirschberg.

The *Yukon Belle*, according to Jack, proved to be one of the best sailing, best handcrafted boats on the journey from Lake Lindeman to Dawson. It would carry over five thousand pounds of outfits, plus the five men of its crew.[9]

The boat building had gone very well, but time was running out. The days were quickly growing shorter. The wind had changed its prevailing direction and began to blow hard in a neverending gale. Much of the time a cold rain fell, soaking the men and the landscape. Everybody's shoes were usually wet and frozen solid each morning. Hands and limbs were often too numb from the cold to work. Despite the scarcity of good, dry wood, a fire was kept constantly burning as a dire necessity.

On the morning of September twentieth, four oars were cut and fashioned from raw logs. Jack exhibited his nautical skills by cutting out sails and rigging a mast and a boom. His obvious knowledge of boats and sailing was already proving useful. Under his direction, the rest of the partners worked as a team to sew the sails for the boats. They all worked until after midnight for they were anxious to leave the next day. The sails they had fashioned with Jack's guidance and help would save them many hours of strenuous rowing. As a finishing touch, a charcoal-based paint was used to place the name of each boat on its stern.[10]

They sailed at noon on September 13. They would follow the generally northward flow of the water on its way to the Bering Sea. They traveled the length of the six-mile-long lake in about one hour.[11] The lake was a narrow mountain gorge filled with water, having a slight "dog-leg" in its middle. The wind was "irregular, blowing great guns at times and at other times dwindling to a strong breeze".[12] Both boats responded well on the water, and the men were proud of their work.

On the northern shore, a small outlet river cascaded into a steep gorge. White waters splashed and skirted around countless large rocks and boulders. It was customary to line empty boats down this river while packing the outfits down the trail beside it. As always, the rope work along the shore was a ticklish, strenuous job. Despite the best efforts of all the lining teams, many boats were damaged or hopelessly wrecked.

According to Thompson's diary, Jack and his friends "portaged" their boats. However, it is much more likely that they lined the *Yukon Belle* downstream, especially when considering that the boat was twenty-seven feet long and must have weighed close to one ton.

Some biographers have claimed that Jack ran the stream, piloting a fully-loaded boat, and then came back to repeat the feat for others. Given the nature of the terrain and

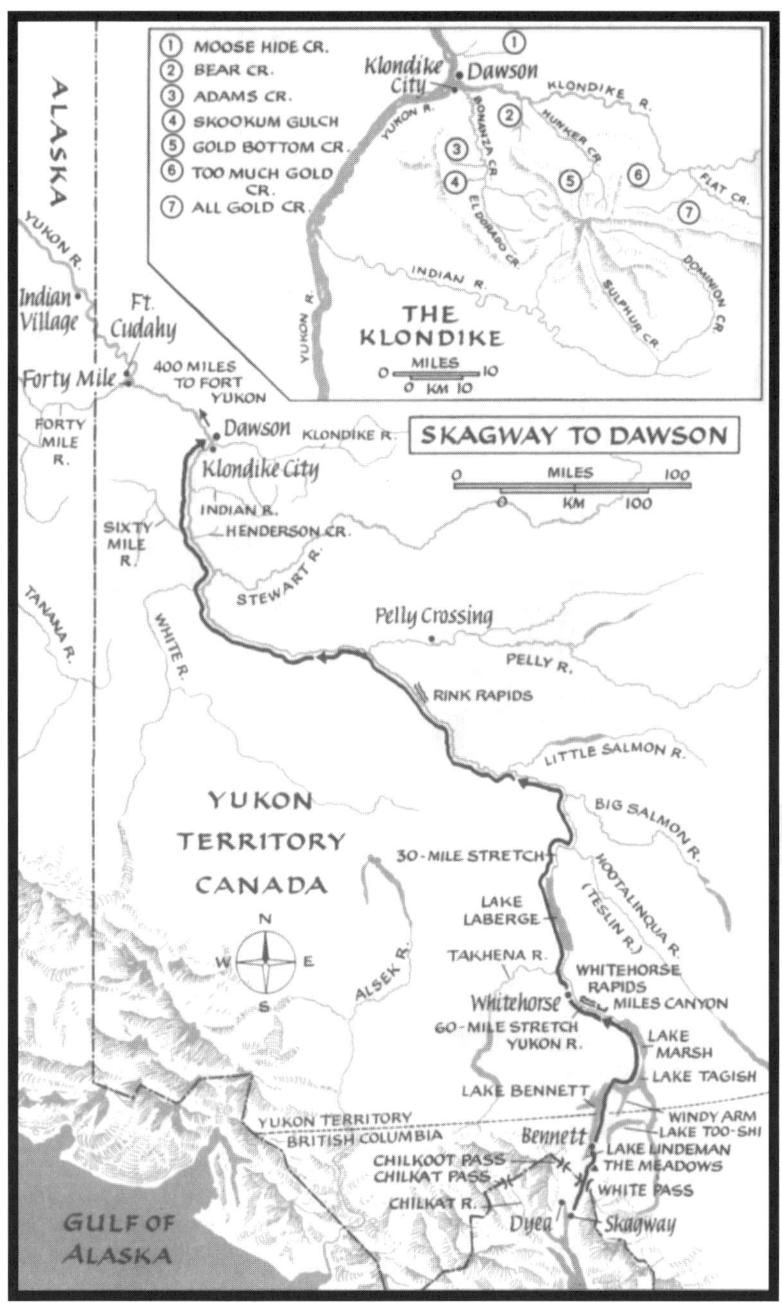

The "Gold Rush Trail" including an inset of the Klondike area.

cascades, it is highly unlikely this happened. This would have been both foolhardy and reckless to even attempt, and would have probably ended in disaster. This also contradicts the account in Thompson's diary which states that the men paid $27.50 each to have their outfits carried by hired packers down the winding sandy path that led through the boulders and trees to Lake Bennett. Packing the outfits themselves would have cost them two days of hard work — two days they needed for lining their boat down the river themselves, taking the greatest of care. In the face of the worsening weather, lining the boats would have been an expeditious and prudent decision.

On the south shore of Lake Bennett, a tent town and sawmill had sprung up that summer, for this was the junction of the trails leading from both Dyea and Skagway. Most of those who came over the Chilkoot Pass Trail from Dyea had already built their boats, though some chose to build their boats at Lake Bennett. Practically all of the travelers from Skagway had to build their boats here. It was a hectic and volatile place, with the pressure of winter's approach being felt more intensely each day.

Jack and his partners did not linger any longer than necessary, but they did hear the latest news — mostly accounts of the piles of dead horses left along the White Pass Trail from Skagway; in fact, there were so many carcasses that the trail was nicknamed the "Dead Horse Trail". There were also tales of dire food shortages in Dawson and in camps throughout the Klondike. Too many gold-seekers had slipped past the Mounties without adequate supplies, especially foodstuffs. Moreover, the sparse Klondike flora and fauna could not support ten thousand additional hungry mouths.

Although many of the accounts of death and starvation were obvious exaggerations, the news was not encouraging. Nonetheless, Jack and his partners were steadfast in their urge to push on.

The crew of their sister boat shared the same experiences, resolve, and haste. On September 22, both crews reloaded their outfits into their boats and pushed away from the shore. They rowed a bit until they could raise their sails, then swiftly crossed Lake Bennett in a very strong wind.

There were many other boats on the lake. To Jack's extreme delight, the *Yukon Belle* passed every boat she encountered, including the *Belle of the Yukon.* But, the strong winds that made the boats speed over the water, straining after their sails, also kicked up waves up to four feet high, making both steering and balancing difficult. Some boats floundered, capsized, or swamped. However, the *Yukon Belle* had the benefit of Jack at its helm guiding it through the choppy, wind-driven waves for the twenty-five mile length of the lake.

Next came Caribou Crossing, the connecting waterway between Lake Bennett and the next lake, Lake Tagish [also spelled "Taggish"]. The link was so-named because of its use as a crossing point for hundreds of thousands of caribou during their spring and fall migrations. Although they undoubtedly saw a few caribou at the crossing, Jack and his partners had missed the main southeastern migration, the brunt of which occurs in early July.

However, they were not there to sightsee. With autumn on the verge of turning into winter, they were racing the natural clock of the seasons. Jack sailed their boat with every ounce of his considerable skill. Everything they had struggled for depended upon reaching their ultimate destination before winter. Charmian London wrote this stirring account of the passage:

> Luck was with him when they came to Caribou Crossing for a shift of wind at the right time sent them humming down the connecting link between Lakes Tagish and Marsh. Nothing could stop them, and Jack, his experienced mittened hands nearly frozen to the tiller he had rigged, held on in high fettle across the menacing Windy Arm, where in a stormy twilight he saw two other boat-loads of men turn over and miserably perish. It was sickening to be unable to lend a hand; but the very law of life in this inimical cold-crystal sphere of the Northland was to keep one's head in just such temptation. And three other souls beside his own depended entirely upon his sailor competence.[13]

At five o'clock that evening, they camped on the shores of Lake Tagish.

Thuswise we voyaged Lake Bennett, Tagish, then Windy
Arm,
Sinister, savage and baleful, boding us hate and harm.
Many a scow was shattered there on that iron shore,
Many a heart was broken straining at sweep and oar.[14]

In the morning, the boats crossed Lake Tagish on the way to Lake Marsh. Between these two lakes the Yukon River began as a sluggish, six-mile-long stream, flowing out of Tagish into Marsh. About halfway along the shore of this stream stood a Canadian Customs House, marked by a red British "Union Jack" flag. This Customs House had been established in October 1896 to deal with the influx of prospectors traveling to the area because of earlier gold rushes and to reinforce the boundary line along the Coast Range.[15]

All boats coming from the south were required to stop there by the North West Mounted Police (later known as the Royal Canadian Mounties). Klondikers had their possessions inspected to see if they carried the required allotment of food and supplies. They also paid a customs duty for whatever they had with them.

Jack and his partners got through this checkpoint by "scheming" (according to Thompson's diary) and were required to pay $21.50 in duties.[16] The authorities were apparently lenient, since Tarwater was allowed to continue despite his incomplete outfit.

After having been delayed for the better part of an afternoon at the Customs House, they were finally allowed to continue. They did not make much more progress that day and camped that night on the shores of Lake Marsh.

The following day was September 24, 1897. On that day, the *Yukon Belle* carried its crew across Lake Marsh and onto the first true section of headwaters for the Yukon River. At that time, this section of river was called "the Lewes" and appeared labeled as such in M. W. Bruce's Alaska. Two hundred miles downstream at Fort Selkirk, the Lewes joined the Pelly River, and from that point on, was commonly known as the Yukon. [Today, the *entire* river from Lake Tagish northward is simply called "the Yukon".]

Thompson and Tarwater cooked dinner onboard as they

leisurely rowed and drifted downstream. After a pleasant afternoon, they camped on the banks of the river for the night. Jim Goodman went hunting and brought back two pheasants.

It was snowing the next morning as they arose bright and early. The weather was noticeably colder. The wind blew stronger, seemingly chilled by the surrounding snow-capped mountains and glacier-filled valleys. This discernible drop in temperature added an urgency to their movement. Soon the rivers and lakes would begin to freeze. It was so cold that later in the day they went ashore to build a fire, warm themselves, and have a hot meal. Jim Goodman went hunting for moose but came back empty-handed. About the time they started downriver again, the snowfall subsided and eventually stopped.

They quickly progressed downriver. By noon, they approached the dreaded Box Canyon. This was a legendary obstacle that had claimed the lives of many Yukon travelers. Here, the river narrowed in width from approximately one thousand to about eighty feet and rushed between the canyon's sheer rock walls, which towered from fifty to one hundred feet above the water. "This enormous volume of water," Jack wrote of it later, "thus contracted to so small a passageway, attains a terrific speed, marked by great boilings and upheavals, and waves which stiffly stand up like walls. By some peculiar action or pressure against the rocky sides, the center of the rapids rises up in the form of a backbone, varying from six to eight feet in height. This is called the 'Ridge'".[17]

The dangerous challenge of this obstacle was compounded by two rough stretches of river that followed directly afterwards: a three-mile series of whitewater cascades known as Squaw Rapids followed by the formidable White Horse Rapids. Though danger was certainly present on the first stretch of rapids, their main concern was the White Horse Rapids, named for a continuous wave of wild whitewater created by a spine of jagged boulders in the river. This wave was known as the "Mane"; its accompanying whirlpool had claimed as many lives as the dreaded Box Canyon. The danger from the rocks through the rapids was at its worst in September, when the lower water levels made more of them appear at and just below the surface. A collision with just one of these rocks could spell doom in a matter of moments for a boat and all on board.

Jack and his partners had to make an important decision: to take several days packing their outfits around the twin hazards or to risk everything — including their lives — and ride their boat through the canyon and rapids. They observed that many others were taking boats through in spite of the terrible risk. Notwithstanding, there were countless stories of lost boats and men.

Jack and his crew walked the length of the trail overlooking the deadly sections. At one point on the trail, above the Box Canyon, they watched and cheered with hundreds of others as boats flew by on the harrowing ride. He fully described the scene years later in Smoke Bellew:

> . . . The Box Canyon was adequately named. It was a box, a trap. Once in it, the only way out was through. On either side arose perpendicular walls of rock. The river narrowed to a fraction of its width and roared through this gloomy passage in a madness of motion that heaped the water in the center into a ridge fully eight feet higher than at the rocky sides. This ridge, in turn, was crested with stiff, upstanding waves that curled over yet remained each in its unvarying place. The canyon was well feared, for it had collected its toll of dead from the passing gold-rushers.[18]

Jack and his partners discussed the situation thoroughly. They were concerned with the snow flurries that had blown through that morning and were mindful of the coming freeze. After the discussion, they took a vote and unanimously agreed to take the chance of running their boat through the rapids.

The risk they were taking must have caused a serious tone to prevail as London, Sloper, Goodman, and Thompson took their positions aboard the *Yukon Belle* in preparation for the ride of their lives. Tarwater would watch from the trail above. It would be his sad task to inform the proper authorities if the men on the boat should perish.

As Jack and his crew shoved off from shore, the strong currents immediately caught the fully-loaded boat. It catapulted into the jaws of the canyon. The best possible telling of the ride comes from London himself:

> Lashing the steering oar so that it could not possibly escape, I allotted my comrades their places; for I was captain. Merritt Sloper, direct from adventures in South America and who knew a little of boating, took his position in the bow with a paddle. Thompson and Goodman, landlubbers who had never rowed before this trip, were stationed side by side at the oars. That the run may better be appreciated, it is well to explain that our twenty-seven-foot boat was carrying over five thousand pounds in addition to human freight, and hence did not possess the buoyancy so requisite for such an undertaking.
>
> "Be sure to keep on the Ridge," cried the men on the bank as we cast off.
>
> The water, though swift, had a slick, oily appearance until we dashed into the very jaws of the Box, where it instantly took on the aspect of chaos broken loose. Afraid that the rowers might catch a crab or make some other disastrous fumble, I called the oars in.
>
> Then we met it on the fly. I caught a glimpse of the spectators fringing the brink of the cliffs above, and another glimpse of the rock walls dashing by like twin lightning express trains; then my whole energy was concentrated in keeping to the Ridge. This was serrated with stiff waves, which the boat, dead with weight, could not mount, being forced to jab her nose through at every lunge. For all the peril, I caught myself smiling at the ridiculous capers cut by Sloper, perched in the very bow and working his paddle like mad. Just as he would let drive for a tremendous stroke, the stern would fall in a trough, jerking the bow clear up, and he would miss the water utterly. And at the next stroke, perhaps, the nose would dive clean under, almost sweeping him away — and he only weighed one hundred pounds. But never did he lose his presence of mind or grit. Once, he turned and cried some warning at the top of his lungs, but it was drowned in the pandemonium of sound. The next instant we fell off the Ridge. The water came inboard in all directions, and the boat, caught in a transverse current, threatened to twist broadside. This would mean destruction. I threw myself against the sweep till I could hear it cracking, while Sloper snapped his paddle short off.
>
> And all this time we were flying down the gutter, less than two yards from the wall. Several times it seemed all

> up with us; but finally, mounting the Ridge almost sidewise, we took a header through a tremendous comber and shot into the whirlpool of the great circular court.
>
> Ordering out the oars for steerage-way, and keeping a close eye on the split currents, I caught one free breath before we flew into the second half of the canyon. Though we crossed the Ridge from left to right and back again, it was merely a repetition of the first half. A moment later the *Yukon Belle* rubbed softly against the bank. We had run the mile of canyon in two minutes by the watch.[19]

After successfully making the run and with their boat intact, Jack and Sloper returned to the head of the canyon to pilot a twenty-two-foot boat through for "Mr. and Mrs. Ret". Thompson's diary notations imply that they did this out of a "goodness of heart".[20] Undoubtedly, it would have been a depressing scenario for Jack and his party to watch these friends die in the thrashing waves of the canyon or to be delayed to the point of being stranded over the winter somewhere in the vast Klondike wilderness. One source states that the Ret's boat was "heavy-loaded" making it more of a challenge to pilot.[21]

After running the Ret's boat through the canyon, the two men returned the *Yukon Belle* to help bail her out. Once the boat was made ready, the crew of the *Yukon Belle* sailed her down through the Squaw and into the White Horse Rapids. Jack vividly described that ride:

> When we struck the "Mane," the *Yukon Belle* forgot her heavy load, taking a series of leaps almost clear of the water, alternating with as many burials in the troughs. To this day I cannot see how it happened, but I lost control. A cross current caught our stern and we began to swing broadside. Then we jumped into the whirlpool, though I did not guess it at the time. Sloper snapped a second paddle and received another ducking.
>
> It must be remembered that we were traveling at racehorse speed, and that things happened in a tithe of the time taken to tell them. From every quarter the water came aboard, threatening to swamp us. The *Yukon Belle* headed directly for the jagged left bank, and though I was up against the steering sweep till it cracked, I could not turn her nose downstream. Onlookers from the shore tried to

> snapshot us, but failed to gauge our speed or get more than a wild view of angry waters and flying foam.
>
> The bank was alarmingly close, but the boat still had the bit in her teeth. It was all happening so quickly, that for the first time I realized I was trying to buck the whirlpool. Like a flash I was bearing against the opposite side of the sweep. The boat answered, at the same time following the bent of the whirlpool, and headed upstream. But the shave was so close that Sloper leaped to the top of a rock. Then, on seeing we had missed by a couple of inches, he pluckily tumbled aboard, all in a heap, like a man boarding a comet.
>
> Though tearing like mad through a whirlpool, we breathed freer. Completing the circle, we were thrown into the "Mane" which we shot a second time and safely landed in a friendly eddy below.[22]

Again, Sloper and Jack hiked upstream and returned with the Ret's boat.

Much fanfare has been made by biographers of Jack's skill in piloting the *Yukon Belle* through Box Canyon and White Horse Rapids. The fact is that many inexperienced pilots succeeded in running these rapids. Survival on stretches of wild whitewater is often a matter of luck, more than skill, especially when piloting cumbersome, overloaded craft. In spite of skill and good luck, the whirlpools and submerged rocks at White Horse Rapids claimed so many lives that the Canadian Government eventually required licensed guides to pilot the boats through safely.

An interesting historical detail to note is that Mrs. Hirschberg was the pilot for the *Belle of the Yukon*. Practically nothing is known about this woman except her name and the fact that she piloted the boat by manning the "sweep" (a long oar used as a rudder attached to the stern for steering). As Franklin Walker related, she was "sturdy enough to wield the steering oar in some fairly ticklish spots".[23] She undoubtedly also captained her boat through the same deadly stretches as Jack.

It is also important to mention a story about Jack which persists to this day in the Klondike. This legend holds that London stayed on for several days at the White Horse Rapids to earn a sizable grubstake piloting boats through the rapids. This story was also propagated by Irving Stone in Sailor on Horseback.

However, most current experts agree that this probably never happened. First, there is no mention of this in either Charmian's or Joan London's biographies. Yet, the strongest evidence can be found in Thompson's diary. His account states that after a good night's rest "with our minds easy", the crew of the *Yukon Belle* cast off for the goldfields again on "Sunday, Sept. 26". This entry indicates that no extra time was spent in that area by Jack London and his partners.

The weather was cold as they navigated the thirty miles downriver to Lake Laberge. [The name of this lake is often misspelled as "LeBarge", as it was on M. W. Bruce's map of Alaska, which was included in Jack's main references to the region.] In the words of Franklin Walker, Lake Laberge would become "the frozen bottom of hell in the saga of the Klondike".[24] This lake was also mentioned in Robert Service's most famous poem, "The Cremation of Sam McGee":

> The Northern Lights have seen queer sights,
> But the queerest they ever did see
> Was that night on the marge of Lake Lebarge
> I cremated Sam McGee.

Never more than five miles wide, the lake extended about thirty-five miles in a due-north-and-south direction. To the great surprise of Jack and his partners, crossing this lake would prove to be the most difficult hurdle on their journey into the Klondike.

The freezing-cold lake had a predominantly steep, often sheer, shoreline offering few good places to land. Compounding the problem of the shoreline was wind — gale-force, bitterly cold, and usually loaded with snow. The snow fell constantly at a varying intensity, from a light flurry to a blinding snowstorm. Buffeted by the powerful wind, the surface of the lake was a riot of white-capped waves, up to four feet high and running in every direction. The shore was an unbroken line of crashing water.

The lake had a very slow current flow at the south end which meant it would easily and rapidly freeze with the first strong onset of winter. To continue, they would have had to sail directly into the gale which was practically impossible.

For the first two days, Jack and his companions sat out a windstorm blowing out of the north. They were soon joined in waiting out the storm by the crew of the *Belle of the Yukon*.

The situation was depicted by Jack in an autobiographical short story, "Like Argus of Ancient Days": ". . . the great gale heralded the freeze-up of Le Barge. Beyond the rapid rivers would continue to run for days, but unless they got beyond, and immediately, they were doomed to be frozen in for six months to come".[25]

Boat-crunching chunks of ice were beginning to appear in the water. This was an alarming sign of the impending freeze that pressed a frustrating urgency upon the stormbound crews.

On Tuesday, September 28, Jack bluntly stated to his partners, "Today we go through or spend the winter here with the rest. We will turn back for nothing".[26] However, the storm continued to howl as the snow piled up around them. They had no choice but to huddle around their fires. Ultimately, they were forced to stay where they were for all of that day and through the freezing-cold night.

The next morning was Wednesday, September 29. The crews of the two sister boats discussed their situation. They all understood that they could be stuck where they camped if the storm continued unabated. In spite of the force of the storm, they unanimously voted to press on.

After breaking camp and reloading the boats, the two sister boats struck out together despite the stormy weather. Since the sails were useless in the face of the gale-force wind, everyone had to row — and row hard — to make any progress at all.

After rowing steadily all day into the force of the blinding snowstorm, they had managed to move several miles north of their previous camp. They were all exhausted but extremely proud of their accomplishment. They stopped to camp for the night at "a very nice harbour".[27]

When they awoke on Thursday morning, they were extremely sore from so much rowing against the relentless wind. Nonetheless, they arose and made a good start early in the day. It was the last day of September.

Before they had gone very far they approached a rocky point. As they came around the point, they came against "a very heavy sea and a hard storm". In spite of heroic efforts at the oars, their rowing proved futile. They could make no headway and "pulled into a little cove under a rock for shelter".[28] They watched in misery as another blinding snowstorm continuously blew for hours. Finally, at four o'clock in the afternoon, they decided to strike out again, presumably because of some abatement in the snowstorm.

Yet, the winds must have still been blowing very hard. Despite an exhausting session of strenuous, nonstop rowing, they had managed to progress only about one mile up the shoreline. There they spied an excellent harbor — a small cove that was sheltered by a gargantuan rock. They beached their boat and camped for the night, hoping the storm would let up.

But, the storm blew as hard as ever throughout the next day, which was the first of October. Sore and cold, they scarcely stirred from their campfires and tents as the wind howled and snow flurries flew. Jim Goodman bravely went hunting alone but "soon returned discouraged".

Early on Saturday, October 2, they again climbed out from beneath their blankets. The wind had completely stopped, the sky was partially clear, and the temperature was very cold. All around them, the magnificent landscape of forests and mountains was covered with a deep blanket of newly-fallen, pure white snow.

The magnificence of the setting notwithstanding, Jack and his partners well understood the great danger they imminently faced. Even in a brief cold snap such as this, the surface of the lake could rapidly freeze. The entire lake could quickly become an impassable barrier, and every boat on the water would be trapped for the winter. The lake would remain impassable until the surface was frozen deeply enough to support a man's weight. Then, an attempt to leave could be made. But, the boats that were caught would have to be abandoned and would eventually be crushed by the ice. Undoubtedly, the prospect of being trapped at Laberge was a grim and impending possibility.

With "a final effort" of determination, they broke camp and struck out. They rowed as hard as they could for the northern shore of the lake which was still many miles away. Since there was no wind at all, the sails were useless, but the water was glassy and placid. Rowing with all their mustered strength, and without the wind and the waves impeding their progress, they swiftly moved up the shoreline.

This time they made good headway. By three o'clock that afternoon, they had reached the northern shore. They entered a river outlet which was an upper section of the Yukon known as "Thirtymile". The pragmatic name indicated the distance to the next major river — thirty miles.

Due to the severe weather, the thirty-five mile voyage across the length of Lake Laberge had taken them one full week to accomplish. Laberge was the last of the lakes on their journey; the rest of the way, they would travel by rivers. They would no longer need to worry about being trapped on a frozen lake.

As it was, they had escaped just in time. Behind them, Laberge soon became a sea of ice and many boats were trapped. Before them, the Yukon River led on to Dawson and "the goldfields" they were struggling to reach.

There was still plenty of danger on the stretches ahead, mostly from rapids and rocks. The ride would be rough for the current was strong.

The *Belle of the Yukon* was still sailing with them, and the two sister boats moved quickly down the river. At about six o'clock that evening, they camped on the banks of the Yukon a few miles upstream from the Teslin River junction. It had been a pivotal — and successful — day in their journey.

On Sunday, they started out early in a cold, dense fog. After drifting past the mouth of the Teslin, they ran aground on Cassair Bar at Hootalinqua. The boat was seriously stuck.

After a tough and bothersome struggle to get the boat clear, they drifted on downstream to the Big Salmon River. There they were barely able to get past the mouth of the tributary river due to the fact that it was spewing huge volumes of bluish slush ice into the fast-growing Yukon River.

As they followed the main river north, another type of ice, known as "anchor ice", began to appear as a coating of crystalline scum on the surface. Anchor ice was often a favorite subject of heated debate among Klondikers. Some believed that the rivers in the far north froze up from the bottom, where the permafrost never thaws. Others believed that the river froze from the cold air touching the surface of the water, spreading at first along the shallower edges, as do rivers further south.

In actuality, rivers in the far north normally run very cold, being fed by mostly ice and snow. Discontinuous permafrost is as common as glaciers. Arctic and subarctic rivers often cut through both glaciers and permafrost. Both can be thawed by the water, but only a glacier will continue to cool the water while the permafrost will not. As winter approaches, the average daily temperature of these river waters dips. As the temperature drops, ice first forms from the contact of colder air with the near-freezing surface of the water.

The "slush ice" Jack and his partners had seen coming out of the last two rivers was composed of small disks of ice formed at the surface of the water called "frazil ice". Frazil ice circulates in the currents as it forms. This frazil ice normally collects and thickens at the bottom of a river. Once these deposits thicken, they often break loose and float to the surface as chunks, giving the illusion of a river freezing up from the bottom.[29]

On Monday, October fourth, they traveled downriver about forty-five miles. At the mouth of the Little Salmon River, they saw more slush ice coming down from Snowcap Mountain, which towered magnificently about thirty miles to the east. Worries about a freeze-up were somewhat abated since the weather seemed to have somewhat improved and the river was flowing along unimpeded.

There was a camp occupied by "a tough looking set" of Indians at this junction of the Yukon and Little Salmon Rivers. These natives were brash and mostly naked, with large rings piercing their noses and ears. Their village was well-situated for commerce, being right along the route of so many gold rush travelers. Seizing upon the opportunity, they aggressively offered fish, hunted meats, and moccasins for sale at highly-inflated prices. Evidently the setup was working, for they seemed to have plenty of money and continued to demand high prices despite the fact that many of those coming down the river, like Jack and his partners, were sensible and refused to buy any of the overpriced goods.[30]

The crew of the *Yukon Belle* shoved off early on October fifth.[31] The weather continued to improve. It was an uneventful day of river sailing until about three o'clock that afternoon when they reached the next major landmark, the well-known Five Finger Rapids.

These rapids were named for a series of five natural columns of rock which jutted above the surface of the water like the fingers of a gigantic hand and divided the river into six channels. Only one of these channels — the farthest to the right — was easy and safe for navigation. Fortunately, word of the far-right channel had been effectively passed to incoming gold-seekers. Armed with this knowledge, the crew of the *Yukon Belle* successfully navigated the rapids without incident, as did most travelers on the Yukon River.

They sailed on downriver and came to a place where a large group of men were slaughtering hundreds of cattle. As the cattle were butchered, the beef was loaded onto newly-built rafts soon to be bound for Dawson. The beef was also offered for sale at fifty to seventy-five cents a pound to passing travelers such as Jack and his partners.

These drovers had learned of the urgent and immediate need for fresh meat in the gold rush area. They had brought the big herd up the Dalton Trail from Haines, a small port town twenty miles southwest of Dyea. In most North American cities, the wholesale price of beef was no more than twenty-five cents a pound; in Dawson, fresh beef sold for as much as $1.50 a pound!

After purchasing some of the meat, Jack and his companions continued another six miles downstream to just past a minor obstacle known as the Rink Rapids. These mildly-rough rapids were negotiated with little trouble by again sticking to the right channel which was commonly known as the channel to take.[32]

The good weather held throughout the long day. That night, they made a comfortable camp along the shore.

The next day was Wednesday, October 6. The weather was good. Now experienced river sailors, the crew took full advantage of the day and covered sixty miles of the Yukon.

They reached Fort Selkirk by that afternoon.

This fort was the Hudson Bay Company's first outpost in the Canadian Yukon. The irreverent gold stampeders loved to quip how the company's stenciled "HBC", found on equipment, rocks, and trees throughout the area, actually stood for "Here Before Christ". When Jack London was there, Fort Selkirk was the primary government post responsible for the vast expanse of wilderness between Chilkoot Pass and Dawson.

With a writer's innate interest in people, Jack must have been intrigued by the crowd at Fort Selkirk, a conglomeration of races and nationalities brought together by the gold rush. Aside from the native Indians, there were Englishmen, Frenchmen, Germans, Italians, Russians, Scandinavians, and Americans, to name just the major groups.

A temporary, informal register was kept at the fort, signed voluntarily by Klondikers passing through the area during the previous two months. Fred Thompson's signature is number 4845.[33] Unfortunately, the register did not serve as an accurate count of the travelers; like the rest of the men in Jack's party, many travelers — including Jack — went by without signing. Nonetheless, the register does provide a clue to the number of people who passed this important frontier settlement.

When Jack and his partners went shopping at the fort's only trading post, there was no food available for sale. This was illustrative of the developing shortages.

There was a variety of animals at Fort Selkirk. Most had been brought by travelers who, like Jack, were just passing through, but a few of the animals lived at the Fort or in the nearby Indian village or camps. There were just a few horses and mules, and most likely some sheep or goats. More notably, there were many dogs belonging to the Indians including malamutes, huskies, and half-tamed wolves. As an animal lover, Jack must have been fascinated.

The partners camped that night at a pleasant spot about six miles below the Fort. On Thursday, October 7, the weather remained balmy. Again taking advantage of the good weather, they started early, and made fifty miles of progress downriver that day.

On Friday, they set out at seven in the morning. Once

again, the weather was good.[34] This was indeed a blessing, helping make up for the time that was lost in the storm at Lake Laberge. Far behind them, the Chilkoot Pass was closed by a violent storm, Lake Laberge was completely frozen for the winter, and thousands of gold rush travelers were beginning to be caught by snowfalls, freezing temperatures, and ice.

As Jack and his partners made camp that afternoon, they discussed whether to stop near the upcoming Stewart River junction to prospect or to continue on to Dawson. They knew their decision could be pivotal to their success or failure in the Klondike.

M. W. Bruce's book, Alaska, on which Jack depended for guidance and advice, highly recommended this area as a good location to prospect. The Stewart River was renowned for its own gold rush back in 1884. It was a small gold rush, not involving great numbers of men, but the two men who originally worked the area brought out over one hundred pounds of gold, worth about $35,000 at the time.[35] The Stewart River Gold Rush had been short-lived, but many old-timers considered the river still prime for a strike and a better bet in the long run than fighting for a claim site with thousands of others downriver.

On the other hand, Dawson was at the heart of the gold strikes. It would be a good place to hear the latest news. There were constant rumors of new gold strikes, and what better place to hear them than Dawson? Based on the information they hoped to learn there, Jack and his partners could deduce the best place to prospect.

Still, they had heard it was not very likely that any worthwhile prospecting locations remained within thirty miles of Dawson. Every possible site for miles had already been claimed.

The persistent rumors that Dawson would face severe food shortages and famine during the upcoming winter also needed to be considered.

With all of these factors in mind, Jack London and his partners — with the exception of Tarwater — unanimously agreed to stop over and to prospect near Stewart River. Tarwater decided to transfer to the *Belle of the Yukon* which was traveling several hours behind them.

The *Belle of the Yukon* was hailed when it appeared. It stopped, staying just long enough to take old Tarwater aboard even though it was late in the day. They immediately shoved off for Dawson. The crew of that boat was concerned; the increasing slush ice in the river was a sign of an imminent freeze.

On the morning of Saturday, October ninth, Jack and his partners first searched for signs of game to hunt. Finding none, they continued downriver. As they drifted downstream, they kept a sharp eye on the terrain, looking for clues as to where gold might be.

At one point, they were passed by thirty-two "Mounties" in several boats. This group was on its way to Dawson to "maintain the right", imposing law and order in the wild and woolly boom-town which constantly threatened to explode into violent anarchy.

At three o'clock that afternoon, Jack and his crew reached the Stewart River junction.

Between the mouth of the Stewart River and the next tributary, Henderson Creek, there was a small island along the eastern shore of the Yukon River. This was known as Split-Up Island [also known as Upper Island]. The name came from the frequent occurrence of partnerships splitting-up there. This was the result of the same decision-by-discussion process that Jack's group had gone through: that is, whether to stay and prospect or to sail downriver to Dawson. After several months of intimately traveling and working together, many partners were simply fed up with each other. Naturally, some partners were not prone to amiable or even reasonable discussion. Unable to reach a consensus, these partners would often separate.

Split-Up Island thus became an opportunity for freedom for partners who could no longer work together. Usually the "split" was fairly amicable, even for partners who had bitterly bickered; but, some dissolutions were so violent and warlike that boats were sometimes cut in half to resolve contested ownership.

Once they had landed on the island, Jack's group explored it and discovered several "old Hudson Bay Cabins".[36] These were probably left by Harper and Ladue of the Alaska Commercial Company.[37] They decided to move into one of these cabins while they were prospecting for gold in the area. If nothing was found, they could always continue to look up the Stewart or navigate further down the Yukon.

They were now eighty miles from Dawson, only a few days of downriver travel — that is, until the river froze. Normally, the river froze in late October, so they figured the freeze was coming very soon. Once the river had frozen and the winter trails had been established, they would again be within a few days of Dawson.

The next day was Sunday, October tenth. They spent the better part of the day unloading, unpacking, and setting up housekeeping in a carefully chosen cabin. Local old-timers they met there assured them that the Stewart was already half-frozen upstream and also had been almost completely staked out. They were told that their chances of finding a claim to stake would be much better if they searched up Henderson Creek, the mouth of which was four miles downriver on the eastern shore of the Yukon River.

On Monday, Jim Goodman, an experienced prospector and miner, went up Henderson Creek to prospect alone. Goodman returned very happy and revealed some small grains of gold he had found.

His find must have been very thrilling to the partners. This was the hope that had brought them all to the Klondike . . . the hope of finding gold.

Jim Goodman resumed prospecting along Henderson Creek on Tuesday. This time he was accompanied by Jack London as well as two fellows they had met on Split-Up Island, Charlie Borg and Emil Jensen.[38]

On Wednesday, the nearby Yukon River was so full of slush ice that Fred Thompson, who had stayed behind in the cabin with Merritt Sloper, predicted it would soon be impassable. Yet, on Thursday, they saw a steady parade of boats and rafts drifting by, despite the increasing ice.

Jim Goodman returned with Jack and the others on Friday. The four men were in high spirits as they happily related that they had all found small amounts of gold. Each had cut and driven at least four corner stakes to define the boundaries of their potential claims. In all, the four men had staked out eight claims on Henderson Creek. One of these claims was Jack's.

On Saturday, October 16, Jack London, Fred Thompson, Charlie Borg, and Emil Jensen prepared to travel to Dawson. They shoved off in the *Yukon Belle* early in the afternoon.[39] They needed to record their claims in Dawson, where the official territorial claims office was located. They also wanted to check for mail and learn the latest news.

On that first day, they traveled downstream approximately thirty miles to the mouth of the Sixtymile River [so named for its distance from the nearest fort]. They found a small trading post with no food to sell, surrounded by empty cabins. A steady flotilla of rafts and boats could be seen coming down the tributary river, headed down the Yukon for Dawson.

They camped for the night at the mouth of the Sixtymile and left early the next morning with two passengers. The identities of these two passengers have never been established.

They traveled all day, stopping only to cut firewood, having learned that wood — even firewood — was very expensive in Dawson. They continued downriver until twilight, stopping three miles from their destination. Since they had no idea what Dawson would be like, they decided to camp at the upriver site instead of continuing and landing in the town after dark.[40]

Early Monday morning, October 18, they set out on the short trip to Dawson.[41] As they floated around a big bend in the river, they saw the mouth of the shallow Klondike River less than half a mile ahead of them on the right, flowing into the Yukon. On the south bank of the incoming river lay Klondike City, better known by its nickname of "Louse Town" because of its infestation by the infamous bugs.

Dawson began on the north bank of the Klondike River and sprawled across a large, triangular flat that lay below slide-scarred Moosehide Mountain. It was bordered to the west by the Yukon River which at that point was a deep, wide, and majestic river flowing northward to the Arctic Circle before it made its big turn west, crossing the width of Alaska. As far as they could see, from river rim to mountainside, was a sea of tents and cabins.

The banks of the river before the city were lined with many types of riverboats — from flat-bottomed dories and scrows to canoes and rafts of every size, all piled high with outfits and equipment. However, there were no paddle-wheeled, passenger steamers in Dawson that fall.

They beached the *Yukon Belle* at Louse Town. Thompson stayed with the boat and their outfits while Jack and the others went looking for a place to camp in Dawson.

First, they took a ferry across the Klondike River. This was a wise way to cross, despite the apparent shallow depth of the river. As Jack and his friends would soon learn, only a week before, old Martin Tarwater had nearly drowned there while trying to cross the river on foot with a pack strapped onto his back. When they reached the other side of the river, they climbed a sixteen-foot bank of loose rock and sand that marked the south edge of Dawson.[42]

Though only one year old in the fall of 1897, Dawson was a burgeoning frontier-style city. The streets were alive, night and day, with gold-seekers of every description, a truly international cross-section of people. The multitude of newcomers mostly hailed from North America, with some from Europe and other parts of the world; hardly any came from exotic cultures with the exception of a few Chinese. Were it not for the presence of the North West Mounted Police ("Mounties"), Dawson could have easily turned out like Skagway, where Soapy Smith and his band of criminals took over the town and did whatever they pleased.

The population of Dawson included an odd conglomeration of gold-seekers, settlers, Indians, Mounties, and just plain drifters. There was a serious but constantly changing corps of owners who ran the saloons and stores. Businesses flourished as entrepreneurs attempted to meet the needs of the throngs in the streets; everywhere it seemed people were hawking everything from scrapwood for fires to mining claim deeds. Outfits of five hundred pounds (without any food included) were selling for a dollar a pound. The fever for gold could be seen everywhere, even in the twinkling eyes of old sourdoughs and the flirtatious smiles of saloon girls. Everyone wanted to strike it rich . . . one way or another. The estimated population of Dawson that fall was about six thousand,[43] which was up from four thousand since August.[44]

As Jack and his companions walked through Dawson,

the streets were bustling with people and animals. Many folks moved about with determination and purpose while others just loitered lethargically. They soon ran into Charles Rand, Dave Sullivan, and William Odette, crew members from the *Belle of the Yukon.* These men told them of Tarwater's close call as well as some of the latest gossip and news.

The mood in Dawson was gloomy. The most talked-about topic in town was the looming shortage of food. Big river steamboats, traveling toward Dawson and loaded with food, had been stopped by the ice at Fort Yukon, over two hundred miles downriver. Two of the steamboats had managed to somehow press on for fifty miles to Circle City, but there they were waylaid and robbed of their cargoes by a desperate, hunger-driven mob.

Just two weeks before Jack and his friends came to Dawson, Inspector Charles Constantine of the North West Mounted Police had posted a notice on Front Street that warned:

> For those who have not laid in a winter's supply to remain longer is to court death from starvation, or at least the certainty of sickness from scurvy and other troubles. Starvation now stares everyone in the face who is hoping and waiting for outside relief.

The general appearance of Dawson was bleak. The town was often shrouded in a chill-inducing fog. Freezing rain, snowstorms, and blizzards were common, and the sky was usually overcast.[45] Although there were days when the sun could been seen, the weather was consistently cold. With the welcome exception of a few attractive structures, most of the buildings were very poorly built; ramshackle shanties and leaky cabins housed the majority of the population.

Nonetheless, many people in Dawson were polite and even cordial. By the evening of their first day in town, Jack and his group had made friends with Louis and Marshall Bond, two brothers from Santa Clara, California. The Bond brothers gave the four men from the *Yukon Belle* permission to set up a tent and camp beside their cabin in town.

In many ways, Dawson was a typical gold rush town. As

previously mentioned, if not for the Mounties, lawlessness would have surely prevailed. But, the Mounties were not overbearing. They well understood the independent nature and demeanor of their Klondike citizenry; they seldom interfered in minor squabbles unless things got violently out-of-hand. As a rule, these authorities maintained a quaint sense of British decorum.

Jack was already familiar with the ways of tough people in rough and ready places. He conducted himself with appropriate caution as he explored the many camps and saloons around town. His favorite activity was to chat with the people he met; his acutely-developed conversational skills were not only noticed but would also be pleasantly remembered.

In fact, there are several accounts of Jack London in Dawson that pivot around conversations. He was apparently willing to broach any subject but loved most to discuss socialism. In his talks around ticklish topics, he raised much more interest than ire. He had a friendly, easygoing tone to his voice and often spoke with an eloquence that left others impressed and practically speechless.

Consider this account by Marshall Bond of a discussion one evening in a Dawson saloon:

> One of these men was of medium height, with very square broad shoulders. His face was masked by a thick stubby beard. A cap pulled down low on his forehead was the one touch necessary to the complete concealment of head and features, so that that part of the anatomy one looks to for an index of character was covered with beard and cap. He looked as tough and as uninviting as we doubtless looked to him.
>
> On a box, out of the circle of light from the lamp, he sat in silence one night, a confused blur of cap, mackinaw, and moccasins. Conversation turned to the subject of socialism. Some of those present confused it with anarchism. One of our number, who at least knew more of the subject that the rest of us, clarified it somewhat with his greater knowledge, but this was soon exhausted. Then from out of the shadow of the lamp, from the blur of beard and cap, came a quick-speaking, sympathetic voice. He took up the subject from its earliest history, carried it on

> through a rapid survey of its most important points and held us thrilled by the hypnotic effect which a profound knowledge of a subject expounded by an exalted believer always exerts. Intellectually he was incomparably the most alert man in the room, and we felt it. Some of us had minds as dull as putty, and some of us had been educated and drilled into a goose step of conventionalism. Here was a man whose life and thoughts were his own. He was refreshing. This was my first introduction to Jack London.[46]

Another wonderful sketch of Jack London in Dawson is included in Edward Morgan's God's Loaded Dice:

> . . . I remember him as a muscular youth of little more than average stature, with a weather-beaten countenance in which a healthy colour showed, and a shock of yellow hair, customarily unkempt and in keeping with his usual slovenly appearance. It seemed to me that whenever I saw him at the bar he was always in conversation with some veteran sourdough or noted character in the life of Dawson. And how he did talk.[47]

For a little over six weeks, Jack enjoyed a "vacation" in Dawson. Many of the things he witnessed and observed would play an important part in his future literary work; most notably, there were the dogs.

Although not as numerous as Jack depicted in The Call of the Wild, the dog population of Dawson was considerable, "a regular capital city of dogland".[48] Horses had not yet been successfully introduced in the region, and dogs were the standard work animal. Just as in his famous novel, the dogs of Dawson in the fall of 1897 were as much of a conglomeration of breeds and mixed-breeds as the people were.

Louis Bond's dog, whose name was Jack, was half Saint Bernard and half Scotch collie. It has been well established that this was the dog London used as a model for Buck in The Call of the Wild.

Half-wolves, such as the main character in White Fang, were present as well, though not as prominently as might be imagined. Wolves are difficult to domesticate. Most wolf-dog mixes were left in the Indian camps where they could be found in abundance and came and went as they pleased. With malamutes, elkhounds, shepherds, and other thoroughly domesticated breeds available, those looking for dogs to work with avoided the less dependable, surly, and undisciplined wolf-dogs. And, in Dawson, a wolfish-looking animal might very well be shot by anyone who mistook it for a wild wolf prowling in town.

It is highly probable that Jack saw man-induced dogfights, usually held outside of town to avoid interference by the Mounties. In these pitched battles, the wolf-dog mixes would have been welcome combatants.

As might also be suspected, prostitution was a standard occupation both in Dawson and Klondike City. It is not hard to imagine that some gold would be spent on ladies who offered the pleasure of their company to the lonely, hard-living men of the Klondike. The fact is that many of the women in the Dawson area had traveled there because of the loosely-spent gold.

However, in London's many Klondike stories, this subject is simply not mentioned. To better understand this, it should be remembered that Jack was writing fiction for a turn-of-the-century reader. The inclusion of prostitution in his already realistic stories would have made Jack's work unpublishable in the eyes of editors.[49]

Since Jack was as comfortable with women as he was with men, he must have been friendly with many of the hundreds of saloon girls, dancers, and "variety actresses" who worked at the scores of dance hall-saloons. The most popular of these establishments were elaborately built and lavishly decorated by Dawson standards, effecting a casino or theatrical atmosphere. These were: the Monte Carlo, the Moosehorn, the Eldorado, the Orpheum, and the Tivoli. Many saloons had the initials of partners in their names, such as the M & G, the M & M, or Pete McDonald's notorious M & N.

However, it was the grandiose Opera House, the only establishment in Dawson claiming to present performing artists for cultural rather than purient interest, which received the most prominent place in London's literature. The Opera House was the site of many elaborate balls to which the guests wore costumes and masks. It was at the end of such a ball, on Thanksgiving eve of 1897, that a fire burned the place to the ground.

Of course, the Opera House was not the only casualty of that fire. Most of the buildings in town were destroyed. This catastrophic fire was reputedly started by a dance-hall girl at the M & N Saloon when she threw a lamp at her rival.[50] Since Jack London was in Dawson at the time, he undoubtedly witnessed this fire and probably helped fight it.

The saloon girls and variety actresses of Dawson's premier dance halls were the town's better-paid ladies of pleasure, often commanding astonishing prices. These and the rest of the women of Dawson whose attentions were available for hire were paid for by the dance, by the drink, by the hour, by the day, and — of course — by the night. Indeed, on any given night at the M & N, the silk-clad, dancing saloon girls were expected to pack in as many as 125 dances, each very short and with a partner who paid one dollar.[51] However, many women were not paid directly or fairly, and quite a few were undeniably exploited.

Prostitution flourished in the ramshackle cribs and shanties of Dawson's skid rows. In his many explorations of the town, Jack must have seen the cynically-named "Paradise Alley" and the spongy swampland called "Hell's Half Acre", both conveniently located directly behind the business district. There was also the squalor of Louse Town, where less fortunate women suffered the unsavory attentions of less-refined men for whatever price they could get.

This type of working woman was well-known to Jack, who had delivered daily newspapers in Oakland's "red light district" before he was a teenager. And, although prostitution was a forbidden subject in Jack's time, he certainly knew both men and women who had been compelled into that type of sexual service, especially when faced with dire economic situations. Behind a facade of pervasive Victorian righteousness, sordid behavior was common but seldom openly discussed.

Saloon girls and actresses were treated with gallant respect and without the mention of prostitution in Jack London's literature. A good example of how he portrayed them can be found in A Daughter of the Snows, his first full-length novel, completed in 1901:

> Butterflies, bits of light and song and laughter, dancing, dancing down the last tail-reach of hell . . . Look at May, there, with the brow of a Madonna and the tongue of a gutter-devil. And Myrtle — for all the world one of Gainsborough's old English beauties stepped down from the canvas to riot out the century in Dawson's dancehalls. And Laura, there, wouldn't she make a mother? Can't you see the child in the curve of her arm against her breast![52]

Even though Jack was careful about directly mentioning prostitution in his literature, many characters in Jack's Northland tales engage in wild and riotous living. For example, in Burning Daylight: the main character loses fifty thousand dollars worth of gold "as a mere ante" in a poker game; McMann "ran up a single bar-room bill of thirty-eight thousand dollars"; Jimmie the Rough "spent one hundred thousand a month for four months"; and, Swiftwater Bill blew "three valuable claims in an extravagance of debauchery".

Although every creek within miles of Dawson had been entirely staked and claimed, there was always the dream that over this or that hill, the gold in some hitherto little-known stream would make a few "lucky" men rich. All that was needed to start a stampede was the faintest rumor of a strike.

Gold stampedes were frequent, erratically jolting life in Dawson. A stampede would typically begin in the middle of the night. As if the news of a strike was possible to keep secret, men would confide in each other, swearing to keep the news to themselves or only to tell their closest partners. In an astonishingly short period of time, everyone in Dawson seemed to know about the "secret" strike. Men would begin to appear in the streets with light "stampede packs" slung on their backs. They would scurry off into the night and disappear, sometimes for several days.

There were very few real discoveries made, and none were very worthwhile.

Unfortunately, every stampede had its casualties. Men wandered off trails, fell into holes, got lost, and froze to death. Quite a few men returned from stampedes with frostbite or nonlethal injuries. There were also trigger-happy and violent miners who wanted to protect their gold, whether real or imagined.

It was probably during one of those mad stampedes that Jack took a sojourn east of Dawson, a dozen miles up the Klondike River, and saw Bonanza Creek, the site of the original strike which had started the Klondike Gold Rush. We do not know this for certain, but his writings certainly suggest that he did. Consider Jack's description of Bonanza Creek from Burning Daylight:

> . . . Late one brief afternoon, Daylight, on the benches between French Hill and Skookum Hill, caught a wider vision of things. Beneath him lay the richest part of Eldorado Creek, while up and down Bonanza he could see for miles. It was a scene of a vast devastation. The hills, to their tops, had been shorn of trees, and their naked sides showed signs of goring and perforating that even the mantle of snow could not hide. Beneath him, in every direction, were the cabins of men. But not many men were visible. A blanket of smoke filled the valleys and turned the gray day to melancholy twilight. Smoke arose from a thousand holes in the snow, where, deep down on bed-rock, in the frozen muck and gravel, men crept and scratched and dug, and ever built more fires to break the grip of the frost. Here and there, where new shafts were starting, these fires flamed redly. Figures of men crawled out of the holes, or disappeared into them, or, on raised platforms of hand-hewn timber, windlassed the thawed gravel to the surface, where it immediately froze. The wreckage of the spring washing appeared everywhere — piles of sluice-boxes, sections of elevated flumes, huge water-wheels — all the debris of an army of gold-mad men.[53]

Jack most likely kept his distance for this was no Elysian vision. This was an image of Hell. This haphazard, every-man-for-himself way of mining was ignorant, stupid, and wasteful. The surrounding hills were stripped of nearly all vegetation and every scrap of wood, giving the normally picturesque region the look of a bombed-over battleground. In addition, this chaotic expanse of diggings was tremendously inefficient; even in this location, where the richest of diggings had been found, it cost an estimated fifty cents to mine each dollar's worth of gold.

By the end of 1898, most of these early mining claims were considered "worked out". However, there was much more gold remaining that would not be extracted until more efficient processes were introduced by big mining firms with trained engineers and tons of heavy equipment.

The freeze-up came late that year. This was a blessing for the many stragglers spread out for miles all over the Klondike. The Yukon River froze for the winter on November 5th.

Coincidentally, that was the same day Jack filed his claim with Dawson's official Gold Commissioner. It was two-and-a-half weeks after he had arrived in town.

For some inexplicable reason, Jack had not rushed to file his claim. It may have been simply because there was a waiting list to see the Commissioner.

The papers Jack filed describe his claim as "placer mining claim No. 54 on the left fork ascending Henderson Creek in the aforesaid mining division".[54] He had claimed five hundred feet of streambed, including the land on either side of the creek "from rimrock to rimrock".[55] Jack estimated the total area to be about 260,000 square feet (about six acres). He paid a total of twenty-five dollars in fees: ten for a mining license and an additional fifteen to file his claim.[56]

Jack London stayed in Dawson for nearly another month. On the third of December, he left Dawson to return to Split-Up Island. He was accompanied by Fred Thompson.

It was a challenging trek over eighty miles of snow-covered trail. Since dogs were owned by only the more affluent or fortunate, London and Thompson most likely packed their goods on their backs or pulled their own sleds behind them as they slogged along wearing snowshoes.

There were many dangerous conditions the two men faced on their journey. For example, there were many places where sheets of thin ice covered water. To fall through the ice and get wet constituted a dire emergency (as in Jack's short story, "To Build A Fire"). The result could be frostbite or death. With the permanent trail not yet clearly marked, it was easy to stray off the track, and getting lost in the wilderness of the Klondike in winter was a potential death sentence.

Winter weather and its consequences were also viable concerns. We do not know exactly what the weather was like on Jack and Fred Thompson's return trip, but we do know that only a few days before, on November 29, a temperature of sixty-seven degrees below zero was recorded nearby. Such severe cold can cause trees to loudly crackle and pop as the freezing sap inside the trees expands. Branches can snap off and fall without warning, landing on unwary travelers (as in "The White Silence"). To touch anything metal would mean losing that patch of skin since the moisture in skin instantly welds to super-cold metal. In addition, the frost at such extremely low temperatures could easily sear a person's lungs. Jack and Fred had to be very careful not to breathe too hard or too deeply; if they did, they might suffer frostbite of the lungs.

Upon leaving Dawson, they first crossed the frozen Yukon River and scrambled over huge, up-ended ice-cakes to reach the western shore. From there, they proceeded south following the riverside bluffs for about fifty miles, often trudging through several feet of new-fallen snow.

To better understand how difficult it was for Jack and Fred Thompson to trudge through the snow, it is important to realize that the snow in the Klondike is different from the snow in the lower latitudes. It is hard, fine, and dry — like sugar. If kicked, it flies and falls with a noisy hiss, like sand. The particles do not stick together when compressed and cannot be molded into snowballs.

Walking through newly-fallen snow in snowshoes was an exhausting and trying ordeal. Jack vividly described it in "The White Silence":

> And of all heart-breaking labors, that of breaking trail is the worst. At every step the great webbed shoe sinks till the snow is level with the knee. Then up, straight up, the deviation of a fraction of an inch being a certain precursor of disaster, the snowshoe must be lifted till the surface is cleared; then forward, down, and the other foot is raised perpendicularly for the matter of half a yard. He who tries

FORM H. 2080

APPLICATION FOR GRANT FOR PLACER MINING,

AND AFFIDAVIT OF APPLICANT.

I, Jack London of Dawson in the Yukon Dist hereby apply, under the Dominion Mining Regulations, for a grant of a claim for placer mining as defined in the said Regulations, in the Henderson Creek Mining Division of the Yukon Dist. More particularly described as placer Mining Claim No. 54 on the Left Fork Ascending Henderson Creek in the aforesaid Mining Division

and I solemnly swear :—

1. That I have discovered therein a deposit of Gold

2. That I am, to the best of my knowledge and belief, the first discoverer of the said deposit ; ~~or~~

~~3. That the said claim was previously granted to~~ ~~but has remained unworked by the said grantee for not less than~~

4. That I am unaware that the land is other than vacant Dominion Land.

4. That I did, on the 16th day of Oct 1897 mark out on the ground, in accordance in every particular with the provisions of ~~sub-section (c) of clause eighteen~~ of the ~~said~~ Mining Regulations, for the Yukon Riv & its tributaries the claim for which I make this application, and that in so doing I did not encroach on any other claim or mining location previously laid out by any other person.

6. That the said claim contains as nearly as I could measure or estimate an area of 260 000 square feet, and that the description ~~and sketch~~ of this date hereto attached, signed by me, setsforth ~~it~~ in detail, to the best of my knowledge and ability, its position, form and dimensions.

7. That I make this application in good faith to acquire the claim for the sole purpose of mining to be prosecuted by myself, or by myself and associates, or by my assigns.

Sworn *before me at* Dawson *in* the Yukon Dist *this* 5th *day of* Nov. *189*7 — Jack London

Thos Fawcett
Gold Commissioner

Form No. 110.

Jack London's actual Mining Application

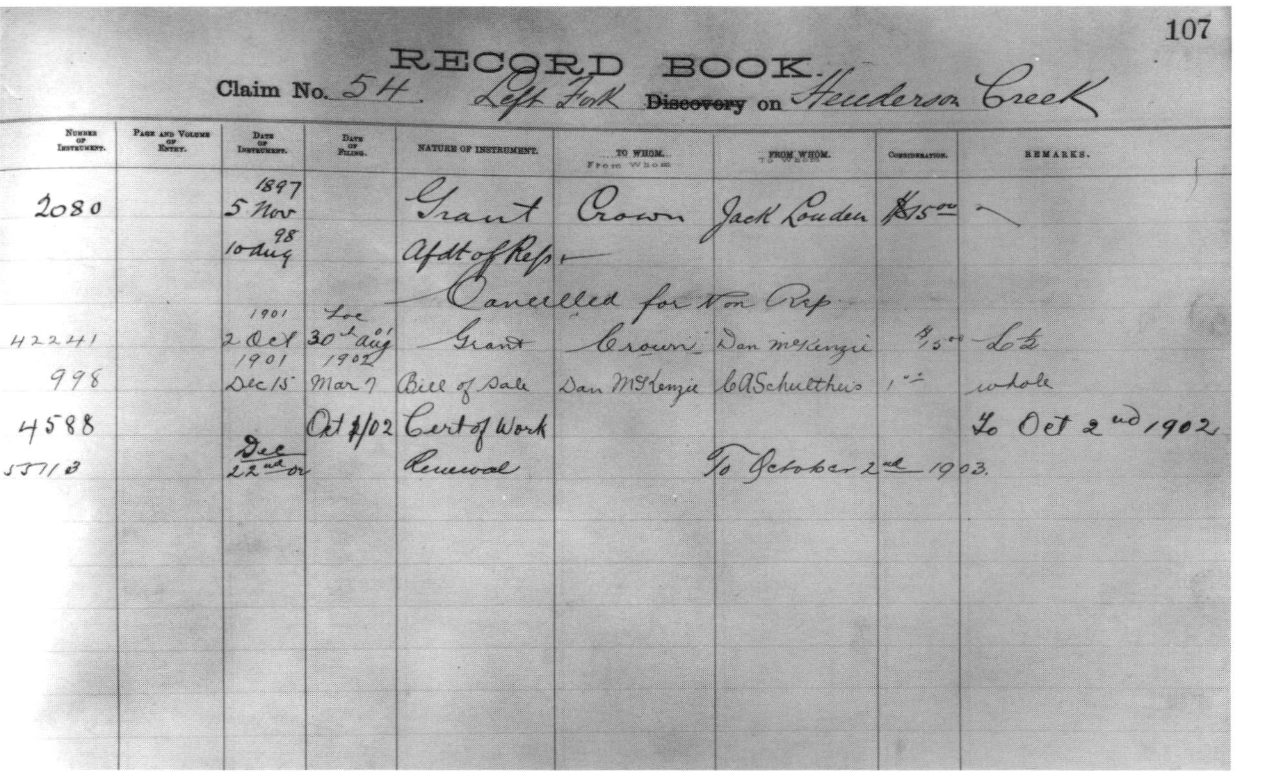

107

RECORD BOOK.

Claim No. 54 Left Fork Discovery on Henderson Creek

Number of Instrument	Page and Volume of Entry	Date of Instrument	Date of Filing	Nature of Instrument	To Whom / From Whom	From Whom / To Whom	Consideration	Remarks
2080		1897 5 Nov		Grant	Crown	Jack Louden	$15.00	—
		98 10 Aug		Afdt of Rep	—			
				Cancelled for Non Rep				
42241		1901 2 Oct	Loc 30th Aug	Grant	Crown	Dan McKenzie	$15.00	L½
998		1901 Dec 15	1902 Mar 7	Bill of Sale	Dan McKenzie	C.A. Schulthies	1.00	whole
4588			Oct 2/02	Cert of Work				To Oct 2nd 1902
55718		Dec 22nd 02		Renewal		To October 2nd 1903.		

The official Canadian Government record of Jack London's Creek Claim and Placer Mining Claim on the left fork of Henderson Creek.

> this for the first time, if haply he avoids bringing his shoes in dangerous propinquity and measures not his length on the treacherous footing, will give up exhausted at the end of a hundred yards; he who can keep out of the way of the dogs for a whole day may well crawl into his sleeping-bag with a clear conscience and a pride which passeth all understanding; and he who travels twenty sleeps on the Long Trail is a man whom the gods may envy.

Attempting to blaze a fresh winter trail without snowshoes would have been even more difficult, foolhardy, and possibly fatal. As they struggled along in their snowshoes, they encountered another jumble of giant ice-cakes at the mouth of the Sixtymile River, about two-thirds of the way to their destination.

For the next twenty-five miles of their journey, sections of the trail had been created by others before them. This allowed them to make better headway. As they neared the Stewart River, the trail again grew difficult as they recrossed the frozen Yukon over yet another jumble of giant ice-cakes.

They arrived at Split-Up Island on December seventh. Their humble little cabin must have been a welcome sight after the challenging five days and four nights they had spent on the trail. Fred and Jack settled in with their partners for the long, dark Arctic winter.

To endure the winter on Split-Up Island, the men settled into routines. Basic survival would mostly entail keeping warm, getting enough fluids and food, housekeeping, and daily necessities. Most of their time was spent indoors waiting for winter to end.

With several men to a cabin, housekeeping was often a full-time chore. The biggest problem was ice and snow accumulating on the floor. This had to be scraped and shoveled out daily. To help keep the floor reasonably clean, a whisk broom was usually kept by the door for brushing off snow, ice, and dirt before coming inside.

Men divided the work to be done in a cabin. These chores would include cooking, cleaning, and laundry. Assignments of chores were often rotated to reduce resentment and boredom. Other skills, such as carpentry or hunting, were also very important. Each man took great pride in his contribution to his cabin's upkeep.

When Jack was the designated cook for his cabin, he learned the demands and secrets of preparing meals for his three cabinmates. Klondike cooks were primarily limited to the "three B's": beans, bread, and bacon. But, Jack's skills as a trader undoubtedly helped to break the dietary monotony. Jack often made visits to nearby cabins for the purpose of trading for something to enliven the daily "grub" (or perhaps a plug of tobacco). Whatever foodstuffs he could swap for — dried fruit or chili peppers, for instance — would bring great delight to the men of his cabin. Indeed, Jack later wrote that if a Klondike cook could incorporate but a few chili peppers into a "mess" of beans, salt pork, and bacon, he would produce "a dish which even the hungry arctic gods may envy".[57]

Men scurried from their cabins mostly during the brief stretch of daily sunlight to do the tasks that were necessary for their survival. They chopped ice from the frozen rivers and carried it back to their cabins in sacks slung over their shoulders. In the cabins, the ice would be melted for water. Wood was also gathered for heating and cooking.

To supplement their limited stores, men went hunting whenever they could. In doing so, they risked their lives for if a man should be injured or lost, searching for him would be very difficult in such a gigantic landscape, covered as it was by windblown and new-falling snow.

Without warning, cold temperatures and bad weather could trap unprepared, unwary Klondikers. Blinding snow flurries could develop in minutes. Lost in white-out conditions, a man could easily wander away from his shelter and freeze to death in the snow. Injuries that would be minor mishaps under normal conditions could quickly become life-threatening when coupled with the danger of the extreme, sub-zero cold.

Very little work was done on the claims during that cold, dark winter. The main reason was that the ground was frozen as hard as cement and was virtually impervious to any type of digging tool. The wood which would be required to thaw the ground so a miner could dig was more immediately needed for the important, compelling purpose of keeping warm enough to survive.

In spite of this, there were some die-hard gold-seekers who thawed, dug, and carried the dirt from their diggings back to their cabins to pan it for gold. But, the amount of gold to be found this way was normally so small as to make this type of winter mining mostly a way to pass the time.

Life inside the cabins was confined and tedious. The interior dimensions of a cabin averaged about ten by twelve feet. Cabins much smaller or larger were rare. Practically all were of the "one room"-style of building. Since as many as eight men could live in a cabin, blankets were often hung to create private areas. Ropes strung across the cabin interiors supported blankets or curtains and also served as impromptu clotheslines, holding everything from socks to salmon. Shelves and pegs on the walls held a myriad of objects, from hats to pots and pans. Wooden bunks and rough-hewn furnishings, such as three-legged stools, were common. A piece of professionally-made furniture was extremely rare.

The ubiquitous "Yukon stove" was to be found in virtually every cabin and was at the center of the "kitchen". These stoves were considered the miner's greatest friend. They were made from one-half of a sheet metal barrel with two compartments, dividing the interior into a firebox in front and an oven in the back. It was topped with a collapsible stovepipe. These sheet iron stoves were packed to the cabins in pieces, then assembled at the site. During the long, cold winter, Yukon stoves were usually kept very hot, often red hot, except when they needed repair or cleaning.

Even with the stove almost constantly burning, there was a coating of permanent frost that clung to the inside walls of each cabin. The frost was thickest down by the floor and reached at least a foot or two towards the ceiling. Men learned to judge the outside temperature by the height of the frost on the interior cabin wall. Frost could also be seen as a sparkling line of white in the "chinking", or space between the logs of a cabin.

Frozen chunks of meat were often stored on a shelf near the floor away from the stove. Although only a few feet away from the stove, these chunks of meat would stay frozen solid. A chunk of meat could only be thoroughly thawed by putting it very close to the stove.

With only two or three hours of natural sunlight per day,

most light to see by was provided by various types of lamps. The best, yet most expensive, were kerosene or whale oil lamps; these were fairly rare outside of Dawson and always used sparingly. In the outlying areas such as Stewart River, the most common type of lamp was the "slush lamp", or "bitch" as they were more commonly called. This was simply a container (such as a sardine can) filled with cooking grease (usually from bacon) which utilized a piece of twine for a wick. These slush lamps gave off a lot of obnoxious smoke and very little light.

The only other light sources were fireplaces and candles. The majority of cabins did not have a fireplace, but candles were used quite often. The drawback was that candles were very expensive — a dollar and a half each — so that their use was strictly limited to necessity or moments of personal indulgence. When men read or played cards by candlelight, they did so knowing the cost. This gave rise to the expression "worth the candle" which means that an activity was at least worth the cost of the candle that was used to provide the light for it.

Since glass panes were rare in the Klondike, the windows in cabins or shacks were usually made of oiled paper, opaque but still admitting some light. These oiled-paper cabin windows were usually coated along the bottom part of their inside surface with condensed and frozen moisture, mostly from the occupants' breathing. Since the windows were usually few and small, even during daylight hours, the inside of a cabin was normally dim and obscure.

Frequently adding to the obscurity in a cabin was the profusion of smoke, primarily caused by cooking, lamps, candles, and stoves. In addition, practically everyone smoked tobacco, which contributed greatly to the amount of smoke inside the cabins.

Like Jack, most of the cabin dwellers smoked as often as they could afford to, which for some was almost constantly. As Hargrave wrote about London, "He smoked incessantly and it would have taken no Sherlock Holmes to tell what the stains on his fingers meant".[58]

Of course, men in the Klondike also chewed tobacco. Being "a man's man"[59] among men who often chewed tobacco, Jack probably chewed a little as well.

The civilized "vice" that men declared they missed the most while wintering in that primitive wilderness was the consumption of refined sugars. In London's own words:

> The cold, the silence, and the darkness somehow seem to be considered the chief woes of the Klondiker. But this is all wrong. There is one woe which overshadows all others — the lack of sugar. Every party which goes north signifies a manly intention to do without sugar, and after it gets there bemoans itself upon its lack of foresight. Man can endure hardship and horror with equanimity, but take away from him his sugar, and he raises his lamentations to the stars.[60]

A more obvious vice that was missed that winter was the consumption of alcoholic beverages. Most men understood the basics of brewing, but many did not have a necessary ingredient — namely sugar (or anything sweet, such as molasses). In desperation, without the necessary sweet stuff accessible, concoctions were sometimes made from anything that was available, usually with awful results. Nonetheless, the occupants of some cabins had constructed elaborate stills. Men impatiently waited and attentively watched as the prized elixir gathered, drip by drip, into a bottle.

In fact, one of the legacies of the Klondike Gold Rush is the nickname of "hooch" for alcoholic beverages. This word can be traced to the Tlingit Indian term "hoochinoo" which was their name for an intoxicating, alcoholic drink.

So it was that drunken Klondikers were rare in the wilderness due to the shortage of liquor, the lack of ingredients necessary to concoct alcoholic beverages, and the fact that many men in the Klondike simply did not drink alcohol. Such was the case in London's cabin where Thompson, Sloper, and Goodman were all teetotalers.[61]

It is probable that Jack consumed very little alcohol that winter on Split-Up Island considering the lack of available ingredients and his teetotaling cabinmates. Visitors to Jack's cabin were never offered anything stronger than "steaming cups of tea".[62]

In the midst of winter, facing the seemingly endless

string of dreary days could also challenge a person's sanity. This could cause "cabin fever". Victims of this socio-psychotic malady gradually succumb to a building sense of frustration which can climax without warning in some irrational act. Cabin fever's most dangerous stage was characterized by brooding behavior and flare-ups of temper. It was a very real malady for men trapped together in a tent or cabin by the harsh Klondike winter.

Joaquin Miller was also spending that winter in the Klondike. Shivering in his Dawson cabin, Miller complained of not seeing the sun for days on end. "Let me not be caught here again," he moaned, "for I am caught like a wary old rat in a trap".[63]

Men slept a lot while the oppressive Northland winter reigned. Except for the few hours of sunlight each day, the cabin was a small spot of warmth and light surrounded by darkness and deadly cold. It was frivolous to venture forth without a real purpose, so men spent most of their time in the cabins. When not pacing about and bumping into each other, men usually stayed in one spot, and very often that spot was prone on their beds.

Isolation and boredom were major problems, and talking was a common solution. Many of the men, like Jack, had never spent a winter this far north. The isolation and boredom that came with the confinement of winter in the Klondike wilderness frequently led to depression. Most men were from cities or towns and were used to socializing frequently with family and friends. Telling each other of personal experiences often diminished the sense of isolation and relieved the terrible boredom. Conversations gave most men a sense of connection to one another.

Of course, talking sometimes meant storytelling. A man could talk about himself or make up just about anything to say, as long as it was interesting. These prisoners of winter were desperate for entertainment, and a good storyteller was worth his weight in gold.

Given his gregarious nature, Jack must have used his natural storytelling ability to entertain his friends on Split-Up Island during the long, cold Klondike winter of 1897. London could spin a cracking-good yarn in a unique, spellbinding way. This skill would prove to be an important factor in his future success as an author.

To avoid the terrible boredom, men also played cards, chess, checkers, or any other game they could think of — anything just to pass the time and stay sane. Of course, Jack had always loved games. He knew many card games but preferred to play cribbage or whist. Chess was his favorite game, and there is some evidence that he put together a chess set.

Jack was so full of life and interests that he was practically immune to boredom. As Emil Jensen wrote years later, "Jack's companionship was refreshing, stimulating, helpful. . . . To him there was in all things something new, something alluring, something worthwhile, be it a game of whist, an argument, or the sun at noonday glowing cold and brilliant above the hills to the south. He was ever on tiptoe with expectancy . . ."[64]

Reading was another very popular pastime that winter in the frozen Klondike. The value of books was so great that the contents of the only lending library in Dawson were kept in a bank vault.[65] Nearly every man in the Klondike that winter had packed in at least one book with him; some had brought in two or three. One miner is reputed to have packed in a complete, six-volume set of Edward Gibbon's The History of the Decline and Fall of the Roman Empire. Men often borrowed books from each other, but in general, books were very hard to come by. Naturally, since there was not much daylight, the cabin-dwellers read judiciously — or paid the price for illumination with candles or lamps.

Being an avid reader, Jack had brought several books with him to the Klondike. Aside from Miner Bruce's Alaska, London's personal library that winter included: John Milton's Paradise Lost, Charles Darwin's Origin of Species, Herbert Spencer's Philosophy of Style, and Das Kapital by Karl Marx.[66] Jack supposedly managed to borrow a copy of Rudyard Kipling's The Seven Seas for Emil Jensen, who found Jack's books too thick to understand and enjoy. By borrowing from other Klondikers, Jack probably had enough books to fill the time when he wanted to read.

Yet, Jack's favorite activity on Split-Up Island that winter was conversation, just as it had been in Dawson. He loved to discuss heady subjects such as the existence of

God, socialism, politics, and philosophy. He was known to be even-tempered, logical, and intelligent as well as a good listener with a ready and winsome laugh. He also loved poetry and could eloquently recite memorized verses.

French-Canadian Louis Savard, a habitually silent but well-mannered and likable man, had the biggest cabin on the island. Louis often played host to several neighbors at once. The cabin's large fireplace was an ideal setting for men to gather around and talk. Practically all of the men from cabins nearby occasioned Savard's more spacious abode.

Jack loved to join the ongoing discussions that occurred around Savard's fireplace. He went there as often as he could.

Bert Hargrave later fondly wrote of the fireside gatherings: ". . . and my recollections of London are intertwined with the many hours we spent together in front of its cheerful light. Many a long night he and I, outlasting the vigil of others, sat before the blazing spruce logs, and talked the hours away". Hargrave continued, giving us this sketch of Jack as he appeared in discussions at Savard's:

> A brave figure of a man he was, lounging by the crude fireplace, its light on his handsome features — a face that one would look at twice even in the crowded city street. In appearance older than his years; a body lithe and strong; neck bared at the throat; a tangled cluster of brown hair that fell low over his brow and which he was wont to brush back impatiently when engaged in animated conversation; a sensitive mouth, but lips, nevertheless, that could set in serious and masterful lines; a radiant smile, marred by two missing teeth (lost, he told me, in a fight on shipboard); eyes that often carried an introspective expression; the face of an artist and a dreamer, but with strong lines denoting will power and boundless energy. An outdoor man — in short, a real man . . .[67]

Because of his quiet nature, Louis removed himself from the ballyhoo of these bull sessions and was instead a good-natured listener. Even if only one guest was in his cabin, he preferred to remain silent and let his visitor speak. When two or more guests were present, he usually sat off to one side, attentively playing solitaire while his guests rambled on. But, on one occasion, after a long and heated debate between London and Hargrave had ended when Jack returned to his cabin for the night, Savard looked up from his game at Hargrave and commented, "You mak' ver' good talk, but zat London he too damn smart for you".[68]

A humorous story about Jack in the Klondike was related by Irving Stone in Sailor on Horseback: "One old prospector who had been caught in a fierce storm stumbled into camp half dead, threw open the door of Jack's cabin, and found it thick with pipe smoke and men all trying to talk at once, bellowing at each other and waving their arms. The prospector reports that when he heard what the crowd was arguing so fiercely, he thought that in his struggles to escape the storm he had lost his mind. The subject of the argument? Socialism".[69]

Whether or not the story is true would be very difficult now to establish. If it is true, chances are that the cabin was Savard's and not Jack's.

Long discussions typically continued — with necessary stops and starts — over several days or weeks during that long winter on Split-Up Island. Many became ongoing debates that could never be fully resolved, usually due to a difference of opinion. For those less congenial than Jack, debates could too easily range into arguments, and arguments that turned bitter often ended in fights.

Of course, fights in that cloistered and hostile environment were extremely ill-advised and taken very seriously. One had to rely on one's partners for survival. If a breach of faith in a partner was caused by angry words or violence, it could prove impossible to mend.

Although most men were able to regain their composures when tempers flared, mutual cabin fever led to the dissolution of many partnerships. However, partnerships sometimes disintegrated with violent, ugly results . . . even an occasional murder!

Even the congenial Jack London was forced to move to another cabin in the middle of winter. The cause of this unseasonal relocation was a dispute over London's misuse of Merritt Sloper's ax. Apparently, Jack had mistakenly grabbed the ax (probably thinking it to be his own) when going out in the dark to chop ice out of a "water hole" (a hole from which ice was chopped for water) at the edge of the river.

Unbeknownst to Jack, so much ice had been removed from the hole that the bottom of the river was about to be reached. As he hacked away mightily at the ice, the blade went through the ice and struck the underlying rocks. The result of hitting the rocks with the ax's steel blade was sparks, easily seen at the bottom of the pitch black hole. Curiously examining the hole and the ax, Jack realized there were rocks at the bottom of the hole and that the ax in his hand was Sloper's. In an attempt at facetious humor, Jack called to his cabinmates saying, "Say, boys, did you ever see ice so hard that it would strike sparks from an ax?"

When the men from the cabin came out to see what Jack was calling to their attention, Sloper suspected the ax might be his and sprang to the edge of the hole. Grabbing the ax from Jack and spotting its badly dulled edge, Sloper immediately launched into a peppery diatribe, but very quickly the below-zero temperatures reminded them all to return to the cabin.

"Why did you do it?" Hargrave whispered to Jack as they hustled back to the cabin.

"Well, I broke off the edge of that ax before I knew it was his," Jack honestly replied, "and I thought that was the best way to let him know it!"[70]

In the relative warmth of the cabin, Sloper "started in on a comprehensive job of cursing". This disconcerted Goodman, who was a religious man. Jack, who could not be offended by cursing, felt terrible about dulling the ax but could not think of what he should say, especially in the face of Sloper's invective attack. Instead, he lit a cigarette, sat back and listened "almost respectfully". But, the vituperous diatribe finally had an effect, and a telltale glint in Jack's eye told Sloper to stop the harangue short of potential fighting words.

This seemingly trivial incident which caused ill will between Jack London and Merritt Sloper is a good example of how cabin fever adversely affected good partnerships.

Furthermore, Jack's original partners may have been miffed at his generous nature, for he habitually invited guests to stay for dinner even if it meant serving less all around, despite "Sloper's eloquent frown and Goodman's mild expression of disapproval".[71] In a place where starvation was a real possibility, dissatisfaction with such a practice is very understandable.

Particularly because of the rift with Sloper, Jack moved into a nearby cabin occupied by three other men: "Doc" B. F. Harvey, a surgeon who had come to the Klondike to get away from alcoholism; E. H. Sullivan, a judge-turned-adventurer; and W. B. "Bert" Hargrave of Colfax, Washington, who would later credit Jack for influencing him to become a socialist. Fed up with the hardships on Split-Up Island, Hargrave moved out of the cabin and downriver to Dawson shortly after London moved in. So it was that Jack spent most of the remainder of that winter in a cabin with a judge and a doctor.

Jack and his new cabinmates proved to be a good team. There were no more serious disputes that winter, and Jack enjoyed many involved discussions with the two older, well-educated men. Old Doc Harvey was so full of colorful stories that he was nicknamed, "Old Thousand and One Nights Harvey";[72] Jack appreciated his new cabinmate's storytelling skill.

It should be noted that Jack's passion for discussion was often given purpose and direction by a voracious mental appetite for truth. As Bert Hargrave later wrote, "He applied one test to religion, to economics, to everything . . . What is the truth? What is just? It was with these questions that he confronted the baffling enigma of life. He could think great thoughts. One could not meet him without feeling the impact of a superior intellect".

Hargrave also commented that he once saw London at the cabin, expounding Herbert Spencer before the judge and the doctor who sat "in his presence like children facing their schoolmaster".[73] This impressed Hargrave for these were learned, much older men who enjoyed Jack's in-depth grasp of divisive concepts.

Apparently, Jack also spent some time that winter at the cabin of Charles M. Taylor. This cabin was situated some distance above Jack's claim on Henderson Creek. The primary evidence for this is an inscription that was found at the back of the cabin on the flat, interior surface of the second log from the top, above the upper bunk.[74] The inscription reads:

Jack London, Miner Author, Jan 27 1898

It has been speculated that Jack stayed at Taylor's cabin during the winter while working his own claim further down the creek.[75] Given the weather conditions, this would have been a very difficult task and one that should have been abandoned until spring unless there were impressive results.

More likely, Jack had simply visited the cabin or stayed there for a very short time since no mention of Jack at Taylor's cabin can be found in any of the existing firsthand accounts. Undoubtedly, a gregarious fellow like Jack would have visited many of the cabins in the area.[76]

Although much of Jack's winter in the Klondike was spent swapping yarns and having involved discussions while sitting in the cabin around a hot stove, quite a lot of time was also spent outdoors. Jack went on many forays, some for just a few hundred yards to the nearest cabins, others for much greater distances.

On one reputed moose hunting trip, he traveled with a hunter (probably Doc Harvey or the man named Mason) and a team of sled dogs, breaking trail for about eighty miles before returning to the cabin.[77] Since Jack hated to kill birds or animals, he would have traveled as a companion to the hunter.

The one time he had gone hunting since arriving in the Klondike, he had shot a beautifully-colored bird for food. Jack was heartbroken and remained haunted by the memory of the bird dying in the bloodstained snow. After that, he simply refused to hunt. Regardless of his refusal to kill an animal, London remained a popular and more-than-willing hunting companion who would help in any way that he could.

Another favorite activity throughout the winter months was estimating the time of day by the use of sticks placed in the snow. In a winter world that often seemed timeless, the passage of time was a comfort, assuring the coming of spring. Jack described how a Klondiker would do this:

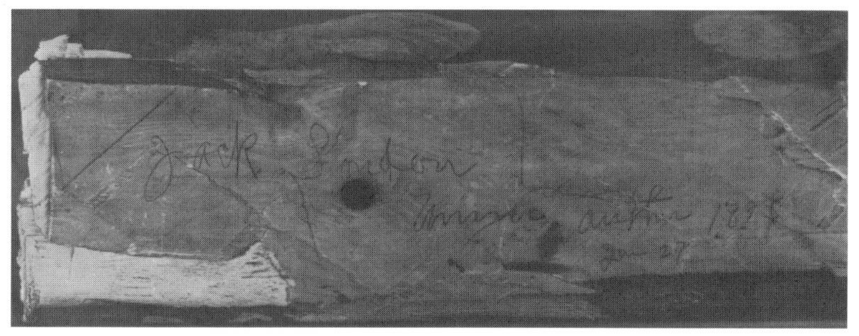

Handwriting verified as
Jack London's *(pictured above)*
found on the flat, interior surface
of a log above the upper bunk in
Charles M. Taylor's cabin *(pictured below)*
near Henderson Creek.

"Before going to bed he wanders outside and studies the heavens. Having located the Pole Star by means of the Great Bear, he inserts two slender wands in the snow to the northward and in line with the North Star. The next day, when the sun on the southern horizon casts the shadows of the wands to the northward and in line, he knows it to be twelve o'clock, and sets his watch and those of his partners accordingly. As stray dogs are constantly knocking his wands out of line with the North Star, it becomes his habit to verify them regularly every night . . ."[78] In other words, the two most important points of a sundial were established using sticks in the snow.

The reader may have noticed that the inhabitants of these Klondike cabins have been referred to only as "men". That is because even though it has been estimated that as many as three hundred people lived in the same general area as Jack during that winter, we know of only one woman.

Furthermore, most white men at that time (including Jack) believed in what was known as "the color line". This is a social barrier created by a difference in skin color. Although there would be "the occasional squaw", these women were of little note to most white men. The one woman who did leave a lasting impression on the men of Split-Up Island did so primarily because she was Caucasian.

Jack London met her when two people — a man and a woman — simply appeared one day at his cabin door. They explained they were from a cabin on the opposite side of the Yukon River. Feeling lonesome and in need of diversion, they had come across the frozen river to visit. They introduced themselves as "Stevens and the Missus". [Researchers still do not know their first names.]

Stevens, the man, liked conversation. He was intelligent, well-spoken, and interesting. He described himself as a transplanted South American adventurer, having spent some time in the upper Amazon jungle. Once they had settled down to talk, he kept the men of Jack's cabin spellbound with bloodcurdling tales of spontaneous killings and rapes. London was thoroughly enthralled. He later described Stevens as "a wild sort of chap, and either a man of marvellous adventures or marvellous imagination".[79]

It was stuffy and smoky in the cabin that day as Stevens wound down his yarns. The focus of the men then shifted to "the Missus". Despite the smoke-besmudged, disheveled look that all of the winter cabin-dwellers shared, the woman was nevertheless attractive. She was twenty-five to thirty years old with wavy red hair and dark blue eyes. Her complexion was fair and freckled. Her teeth were small and white, gleaming between her "red-blooded, rather sensuous lips".

Missus Stevens was a little plump and decidedly buxom, with a full, well-rounded figure. This was particularly exposed by her tight, dilapidated dress once she had removed her layer of cold-weather outer garments. And, although it was unreservedly frank, her seductive, feminine voice filled the cabin like music as the men who surrounded her listened and hung on her every word.

She told them that she had come to the Klondike because of a message from a "control" in the spirit world. This "control" spirit had assured her that she would be led to untold riches in the far north. Pausing for a moment, she ran her hands through her unruly hair and threw back her head, languishing with a satisfied smile in the limelight of the flattering attention.[80]

Just as Jack had been enthralled by her companion's tales of adventure, she was obviously enchanted by Jack, who was a young, handsome, and strongly-built youth undeniably "much at ease before women". She continually glanced appraisingly at him. At one point, she offhandedly volunteered that "she had no legal right to the name" of Stevens. This probably meant that she and her male companion were not married. Surely, the meaning of the statement was not missed by the men in the room.

After the couple left Jack's cabin, there was considerable talk regarding them. There was doubt of Stevens' truthfulness, and the woman was clearly a hussy. Nevertheless, Jack liked the stories of jungle adventures and was intrigued by the buxom mistress.

When Jack announced that he would like to visit the Stevens' cabin, Emil Jensen warned him that "baby eyes in a woman of her age spells trouble". Of course, this warning did nothing to deter Jack from crossing the frozen river a few days later for more wild-eyed tales . . . and to once again see the woman!

Stevens did not disappoint London when it came to spinning more tales of adventure. In fact, he outdid his previous performance and continued for several hours while his mistress coyly watched in silence. When Stevens finally ran out of steam, his female companion saw her chance to speak directly with Jack, repeating that her presence in the Klondike was because of her experiences with spiritualists. One wonders how Jack London reacted to this declaration since his mother considered herself to be a spiritualist medium, and he was known to openly scoff at such assertions.

The woman's attraction to London must have become noticeable for suddenly Stevens interrupted her account. Staring at Jack with his small, beady eyes, Stevens asked in a cold, even voice, "Have you even seen straight shooting, Mr. London?" Without waiting for his guest to reply, he arose from the edge of the bed where he had been sitting and removed a Winchester rifle from its hook above the stove.

Without a word between the two men, they arose and stepped out into the snow together. Stevens nailed a piece of tin to a tree near the trail. After returning to where Jack stood, he proceeded to give Jack a demonstration of his shooting skills by placing ten shots into the small metal target "in a matter of seconds". The unspoken message was clear, and Jack soon excused himself from the visit.

On returning to his cabin, an obviously impressed Jack told his cabinmates, "That man has an eye as quick as thought and muscles as flexible as steel. He is afraid of nothing. Of nothing, I tell you, not even the truth . . ."

As far as we know, Jack London did not visit the Stevens' cabin again.[81]

Jack had many qualities that made him very well liked and memorable to everyone in the Klondike who met him. Those who would later describe him would typically do so with remarkably glowing praise. Among the impressive accolades from these honest, well-seasoned men of the Klondike are the following:

Emil Jensen wrote, “I never tired of his companionship”.[82] W. B. Hargrave related:

> It was in October of 1897 that I first met him. . . . No other man has left so indelible an impression upon my memory as Jack London. He was but a boy then, in years, but he possessed the mental equipment of a mature man and I have never thought of him as a boy except in the heart of him . . . the clean joyous, tender unembittered heart of youth. His personality would challenge attention anywhere. Not only in his beauty — for he was a handsome lad — but there was about him that indefinable something that distinguishes genius from mediocrity, he displayed none of the insolent egotism of youth; he was an idealist who went after the attainable, a dreamer who was a man among strong men; a man who faced life with superb assurance and who could face death serenely imperturbable. These were my first impressions which months of companionship only confirmed.
>
> He was intrinsically kind and irrationally generous . . . With an innate refinement, a gentleness that had survived the roughest of associations. Sometimes he would become silent and reflective, but he was never morose or sullen. His silence was an attentive silence. . . . He was always good-natured; he was more — he was charmingly cheerful.[83]

And, B. F. “Doc” Harvey once told Hargrave, “After you, I’d rather have Jack London for a partner than any man on the river”.[84]

In addition to Jack’s partners and those people who have previously been mentioned, there were other men who are known to have spent that winter in the Split-Up Island area and who were acquainted with Jack London. Many of these men, their names, or parts of their names would appear in London’s future writing. There was a man from eastern Oregon named Elam Harnish (whose nickname was “Burning Daylight”). There were Harnish’s partners: a German named Charlie Meyers, a nameless Swede, and a nameless French-Canadian. Others included: Charles M. Taylor, a Kentuckian who had attended Annapolis; William (“Will”) Harrington, a football star from Stanford University; Cornelius “Con” Gepfert, Clarence Buzzini, and Everett

Barton, all of whom corresponded with London after London's return from the Klondike; John Dillon; W. Casswell Prewitt; Charley Meadow, known as "Arizona Charley"; Hank Putnam, a professional gambler; Sam Adams; Del Bishop, a pocket-miner who became one of the leading characters in London's book, A Daughter of the Snows; W. T. Peacock, a Texas cowboy, whose name was the basis for Bill Peabody in Smoke Bellew; and big-hearted John Thorson who was the inspiration for Buck's master, prospector John Thornton, in The Call of the Wild.

Other men who lived in the area we know only by partial names or nicknames. These men include: Wolf the Malignant, who fought every day with his three unnamed partners; Carthy (or Courthé); and Keough, who was known as "the giant Irishman" and whose actual name may have been Key Pittman.[85]

There were plenty of dogs around Split-Up Island, though none of them belonged to Jack. Still, he made friends with animals easily, and it is safe to assume he would have been at ease with most of the dogs that lived there that winter. One canine we know of was Louis Savard's dog, probably a black Labrador Retriever, who Emil Jensen wrote of as "lovable Nig, the short-haired, outside dog".

Charmian London described an incident that illustrated Jack's affection for dogs. Savard had taken Nig with him on a long trek up the banks of the Sixtymile River. When the dog saw his master preparing to leave and the heavily laden sled he was expected to pull, he ran off. After returning to the Split-Up Island cabin, an infuriated Savard threatened to kill the dog when it returned. Only Jack's "eloquent appeal" saved the dog from destruction.

Of all the "outside dogs" in the area, Newfoundlands and St. Bernards were preferred and most common; but, one could find a wide variety of breeds and mixed breeds, including many short-haired dogs like Savard's. In an article written years later for "Harper's Weekly", Jack spoke of the Eskimo dogs and commented on their methods of getting water to drink in the frozen outdoors. "It is a very common sight to see these animals breaking the ice of a water-hole," he wrote, "by rearing in the air and coming down upon it with their whole weight on their fore feet".[86]

As good fortune would have it, the main trail from the outside world into the Klondike followed along the eastern shore of the Yukon River not far from Split-Up Island. Jack most likely witnessed the breaking of the trail with a sled when Andrew Flett, a Mackenzie River half-breed, brought the first mail of winter in January using a four-dog team of huskies. A little later that winter, Canadian Mounties driving forty of "the Queen's dogs" also passed Split-Up Island with the first big load of mail going north. Later that winter, Pat Galvin proved that his husky team was one of the best in the Yukon when he carried the first load of outgoing mail from Dawson to Fort Selkirk in an astonishing run of 175 miles in three-and-one-half days — an average of fifty miles a day![87]

Many others passed through the Split-Up Island area on the main trail that winter. Seeing and meeting many of these travelers, Jack undoubtedly gained a great appreciation for the spirit of those who could and would brave the sub-zero weather, facing seemingly endless snow and ice, dangerous pitfalls, and incredible fatigue. Certainly, the achievements of these men who prevailed so well against nature would not have been lost on the perceptive, fledgling young writer. Jack's insight into and appreciation of them are evident in a toast given by the main character in one of London's first published Klondike stories, "To the Man on Trail":

> A health to the man on trail this night; may his grub hold out; may his dogs keep their legs; may his matches never miss fire.

Jack understood the rigors of a fresh winter trail in the Klondike, for he had broken such a trail himself, both in snowshoes and with dogs. He had spent a full day traveling on a snowy trail and slept beneath a fly tent on a mattress of freshly-cut conifer branches (used for comfort and insulation), warmed within the life-giving reach of a well-built fire.

Jack also found a marvelously random cross-section of men in the cabins and camps surrounding his own. This variety in personality types gave the young writer a unique opportunity to observe human nature exposed in raw, demanding situations. He had time to analyze the various ways in which men reacted to one another in triumph, under stress, and in boredom. He witnessed the limits of strength, resourcefulness, and friendship as well as the pitfalls of weakness, petty selfishness, and hostility. He saw how most men accepted the situation and made themselves as amicable as possible to get through the challenges of that rugged environment.

Compared to what he had seen in cities across the United States, Jack noticed that men seemed larger in the wilderness. In the cities, men were controlled and directed by others who were primarily concerned with power and profit. But, in the wilds, Jack discovered another type of man, out of the reach of the oligarch's grasp, adapting to the whims of nature. Many of these men would grow to legendary proportions by right of their deeds in the face of a vast, unforgiving landscape where survival was an everyday skill.

Although there were many unsung heroes who overcame the challenges of that hostile environment, there were also many casualties. Burns from fires and frostbite were common. Broken bones or serious lacerations could easily become a life-threatening crisis. There were also many diseases in the Klondike that winter including common colds, influenza, pneumonia, chicken pox, gonorrhea, syphilis, meningitis, and scurvy.

Emil Jensen related an interesting life-and-death incident concerning Jack London and Charlie Borg. [Borg and Jensen had accompanied Jack on his original prospecting trip up Henderson Creek.] Apparently, Charlie had broken his ankle while crossing the Chilkoot Pass. He had tried to set the break himself and believed it was set; but, evidently he had done something wrong. Despite the fact he was able to use it for awhile, during the long winter complications developed and the foot had grown swollen, painful, and discolored. Shortly after he became one of Emil Jensen's cabinmates, the pain in Charlie's foot became so severe that Doc Harvey was asked to come over and examine it.

After looking at Borg's foot, Old Doc Harvey declared that if the foot was not amputated, Charlie would die — probably from a deep-seated, gangrenous infection. But, the extreme pain of an unanesthetized amputation could also kill a man. Since Doc Harvey had come to the Klondike to prospect, to get away from alcohol, and not to practice medicine, he had very few medical tools and no anesthetics with him.

After a frantic and thorough search of all the nearby camps and cabins, no painkillers could be found. However, in his personal medicine chest, Jack London had a one-quart bottle of whiskey. He had carried that bottle all the way from Oakland to Split-Up Island. It had never been opened. He had kept it faithfully in reserve for some momentous occasion or dire emergency. When no better anesthetic could be found to ease the pain of Charlie Borg's amputation, Jack immediately donated his bottle of whiskey.[88]

After all other preparations for the operation had been completed, the bottle of "anesthetic" was opened. First, one quarter of the bottle went down Doc Harvey's throat to "steady his nerves". As Doc savored the taste and felt the impact of the drink, he declared it very good whiskey and passed the jug to his patient. The doctor instructed his patient to finish it off quickly, and the patient dutifully obeyed. As soon as it became apparent that Charlie was patently drunk, the operation began.

It was a cruel and sickening spectacle according to Jensen who later declared in his memoirs, "Thanks to the benumbing effects of that whisky, my partner survived the butchering . . ."[89] Years later, Jack London received a touching letter of thanks from Charlie Borg and his family.

The many long months of winter continued until it seemed as if winter would never end. Outside the cabins, the snow averaged about four feet in depth although storms, drifts, and pockets could make it much deeper.[90] Throughout December, January, February, March, and April, those living in the cabins on Split-Up Island did what they could to endure and survive the long ordeal.

By May, the sun was shining brightly for several hours a day. The buds were forming on the trees and signs of the coming spring were just beginning to appear. However, many of the men were contending with scurvy, a disease caused by a deficiency of vitamin C and known as "the scourge of the North".

Jack developed one of the most serious cases in the area. First, his gums had become spongy. Next, he became tired and listless. Then, his teeth began to loosen and his weariness increased.

The cause of Jack's problems was well understood, but no one on the island could help him; all the dried fruits and canned vegetables had long since been consumed. The other men of the island were sympathetic to Jack's condition but not far behind him in succumbing to the same disease, including his cabinmate, Doc Harvey.

The old-timers' remedy for scurvy was spruce needle tea; however, its content of Vitamin C was minuscule. Even when drank in copious quantities, the tea was not potent enough to cure or even curb an advanced case of the disease. Until fresh, vitamin C-containing foods could be found, Jack could only hope to delay the worsening effects of the disease by drinking as much spruce needle tea as he could. The tart-tasting beverage was probably drunk unsweetened due to the shortage of sugar and sweeteners.

Everyone on Split-Up Island was delighted that spring was coming, as was Jack, but he was also very concerned about his scurvy. His condition was quickly worsening. His face became puffy, and his limbs were becoming both swollen and spongy. Using his finger, Jack could press a dent into his doughy arm and watch in quiet dismay as the dent lingered in the skin for an unnaturally long time, refusing to go away. His joints began to ache severely, and his feet became constantly sore.

Undoubtedly, Doc Harvey explained to Jack what he could expect if his scurvy continued to progress and he did not get treatment soon. His legs were already beginning to buckle and go lame. Next, his skin would become incredibly dry and rough, eventually to be mottled with ugly patches of red, blue, and black. His gums would continue to swell and bleed. His teeth would rattle in their sockets and soon thereafter fall out. His breath would carry a horrible stench. His face would turn a waxy yellow and have a perpetually leaden expression. His eyes would sink deep into their sockets as he became a living skeleton. Finally, he would painfully die.

Death in the Klondike was especially common during the great gold rush of 1897-98. The harshness of the climate and the hardships of the trail took a dreadful toll on the inexperienced, unprepared, and unlucky ones among the many thousands of gold-seekers. Cemeteries sprang up almost as quickly as towns and settlements. At least, those dead received a somewhat proper burial; many prospectors who died in more remote locations did not. Many people simply disappeared.

Death could also be attributed to other causes. Between the years 1896 to 1900, hundreds of bodies and unmarked graves were discovered along the rivers and trails of the Klondike. Suicides occurred on a regular basis. Partners were also known to have killed one another, so that only their bodies, their bones, or their absence spoke of the fate that befell them. And, as mentioned previously, men went mad with cabin fever — sometimes with fatal consequences.

In the Northland tales Jack London would later write, many of the characters faced an untimely death. His literature was an accurate reflection of the mortality rate and the causes of death familiar to the men and women who participated in the Klondike Gold Rush.

In "The White Silence", one of Jack's first published Klondike tales, a man named Mason was severely injured by a falling tree while traveling on a winter trail with his Indian wife and a male partner. Jack depicted the scene realistically:

> . . . Mason toiled on at the head of the cavalcade, little dreaming that danger hovered in the air. The timber clustered thick in the sheltered bottom, and through this they threaded their way. Fifty feet or more from the trail towered a lofty pine. For generations it had stood there, and for generations destiny had had this one end in view, — perhaps the same had been decreed of Mason.
>
> He stooped to fasten the loosened thong of his moccasin. The sleds came to a halt and the dogs lay down in the snow without a whimper. The stillness was weird; not a breath rustled the frost-encrusted forest; the cold and silence of outer space had chilled the heart and smote the trembling lips of nature. A sigh pulsed through the air, — they did not seem to actually hear it, but rather felt it, like the premonition of movement in a motionless void. Then the

> great tree, burdened with its weight of years and snow, played its last part in the tragedy of life. He heard the warning crash and attempted to spring up, but almost erect, caught the blow squarely on the shoulder.

Mason "was terribly crushed". His partner and his wife made a heroic effort to comfort and encourage him but soon had to face the obvious and inevitable conclusion that if they were to survive, Mason must be left behind to die.

In another of Jack's future short stories, "The League of the Old Men", a man was discovered sitting upright, frozen to death in a sled that was parked on the main street of Dawson. The dead man had been there for hours. Many people who had passed him assumed he was resting. After the shock of the discovery, it was decided to bury the man. But, in order to get the man's body to lie down flat in a coffin, they had to thaw him out. Chances are this incident actually happened, and Jack either witnessed it or heard about it while visiting Dawson.

One of the most dreaded tasks in the Klondike, aside from thawing out frozen bodies, was digging a grave. Out on the trail, a pile of rocks would often be deemed sufficient. In the settlements and communities, as previously mentioned, at least some effort was made to properly bury the dead. In Dawson, the most developed city in the Klondike, the deceased were usually placed in a coffin, despite the chronic shortage of wood.

Because of the frozen ground, digging a grave in the Klondike in winter was an exhausting and tedious ordeal. It was terribly hard, disheartening work often conducted in the bitterest cold.

Graves dug during those gold rush winters were seldom more than two feet deep but could easily take an entire day to dig. The ground was frozen as hard as concrete and had to be thawed one inch at a time. This was done by building a fire over the gravesite and then quickly brushing away the cinders in order to dig. When the thawed earth had been removed or refroze, the entire process would be repeated. In this manner, a grave could be dug at the rate of two or three inches an hour.

Adding to the difficulty of the situation was the weather

— often sullen, cold, and foggy with a freezing mist or rain. It regularly snowed. Sometimes a punishing wind would blow. All of this encouraged the funeral entourage, and especially the gravediggers, to quickly finish the unpleasant task and get back to a warm fireside. But, if the task was insufficiently done, parts of the recently-buried body would soon be seen lying about nearby. This was a sign that the body had been dug up by scavengers, usually sled dogs or wolves.

Jack had no doubt seen bodies and graves along the way to Dawson. He had witnessed at least one proper burial there in the fall of 1897.[91]

With all of this morbid knowledge in his mind, young Jack London watched the giant ice-cakes that covered the Yukon River, waiting for the full-blown arrival of spring as April drew to a close. If the breakup of the ice-cakes on the river did not come soon, he knew that Split-Up Island would be where he died.

Maintaining his typically cheerful demeanor, Jack faced his death in the Klondike. There were hundreds, if not thousands, of others like Jack scattered throughout the Klondike enduring the effects of worsening scurvy. This dire situation is depicted with eloquence and understanding by Robert Service in his famous poem, "The Law of the Yukon":

> This is the Law of the Yukon, that only the strong shall
> thrive;
> That surely the Weak shall perish, and only the Fit survive.
> Dissolute, damned and despairful, crippled and palsied
> and slain,
> This is the Will of the Yukon — Lo, how she makes it plain!

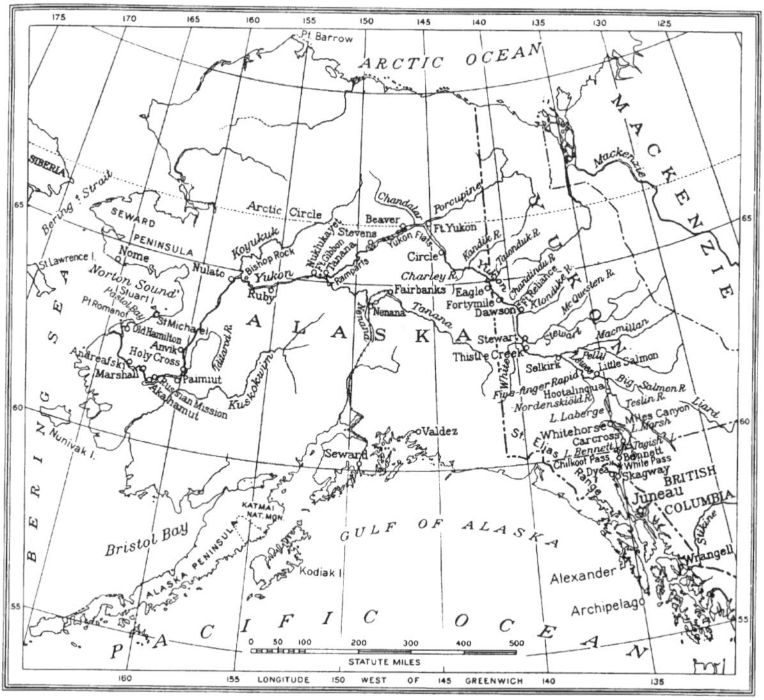

Map detailing the Northland Region Jack London traversed during his Klondike adventure. *Map by A. H. Bumstead*

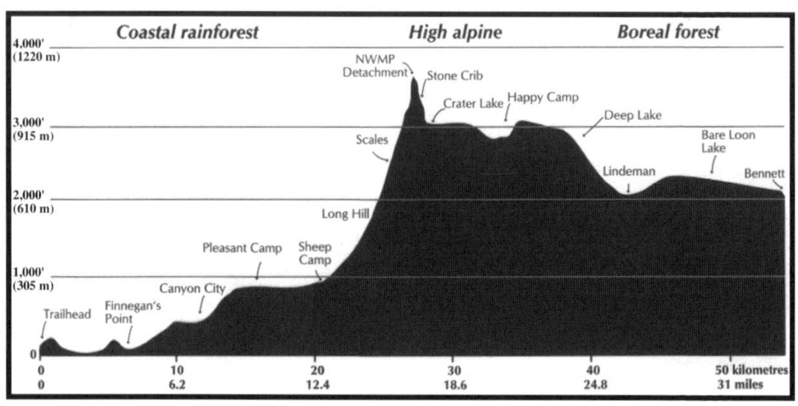

Chart detailing camps and ecozones of the Chilkoot Trail. *Based on illustrations from the Department of Canadian Heritage and the U.S. National Park Service.*

Chapter Three

The Long Journey Home

Jack felt compelled to leave Split-Up Island because of his scurvy. It was vital that he travel to Dawson as soon as the river was passable. If he stayed where he was, his condition would most likely worsen, he would die, and he would be buried on Split-Up Island. If he traveled to Dawson, he had a good chance of finding treatment and saving his life.

Jack apparently had no problem leaving his claim. He had talked with the experienced men around him and understood that although there was gold on his claim, the deposits were not rich enough to warrant the physical efforts of mining. He also knew that he could make more money per hour employed on a ship as a sailor, and the labor would be easier than working his claim.

Throughout April, fierce storms had raged as if to announce that winter was refusing to leave. Nevertheless, in early May, the river began to thaw. Jack described this scene in A Daughter of the Snows:

> So summer waited for open water, and the tardy Yukon took to stretching of days and cracking its stiff joints. Now an airhole ate into the ice, and ate and ate; or a fissure formed, and grew, and failed to freeze again. Then the ice ripped from shore and uprose bodily a yard. But still the river was loth to loose its grip. It was a slow travail, and man, used to nursing nature with pigmy skill, able to burst waterspouts and harness waterfalls, could avail nothing against the billions of frigid tons which refused to run down the hill to the Bering Sea. On Split-Up Island all were ready for the break-up.[1]

As the ice broke up with loud cracks and pops, countless fragments — from bigger than a house to mere slush — began jostling along in the current, only to be stopped by an ice jam further downriver. The unremitting thaw would increase the backwash of water and ice until the jam could no longer hold; it would break, allowing the downstream procession of water and ice to continue until another jam occurred.

None of the men who had wintered on the island planned to remain. One good reason to get off the island was that all of the claims in the area were considered to be poor. Furthermore, the gold deposits were not easy to mine. Another reason was the inevitable, monstrous ice-cakes which were expected to come tumbling downstream and severely damage the island. Small islands in the Yukon River were annually denuded and deformed as the spring thaw broke up the ice, sending countless massive ice chunks toward the sea with all of the hydraulic force created by the mighty, rampaging river. In fact, some islands had been utterly obliterated in past spring floods.

All the men on Split-Up Island moved their belongings to much higher ground. They then watched the incredible spectacle of the breakup from the safety of the hillsides and bluffs overlooking the river. An increasingly dramatic suspense prevailed as they waited for the breakup to begin in earnest.

After the thaw produced navigable waters, some men were figuring on going upriver, while others, like Jack, were planning to travel downstream towards Dawson. Most of the men in the area were afflicted with scurvy to some degree. There were also many minor injuries and discomforts that could use good medical attention; most had gone untreated during the long, harsh winter. Compounding the effect of so much physical misery was the fact that most men were simply homesick and tired of living in the Klondike. The wait must have been especially poignant for Jack, whose life depended upon the river opening soon.

This situation gave Jack ample opportunity to reflect on his life, and the threat of certain, impending doom obviously helped him to focus his thoughts. Thinking about all he had done and how much more he would like to do, London must have reflected on the conversations and storytelling in which he had participated, whiling away the hours during the bleak winter.

For the past three years, Jack had pursued an elusive dream to become a professional writer. He obviously had a natural gift for communicating his ideas and experiences. Now, as he waited on the banks of the Yukon for the lifesaving thaw, Jack London must have considered that he *should* be a writer, especially a teller of tales.

Throughout the first part of May, late winter storms kept the river impassable and delayed the anticipated thaw. It was not until the last week of the month that winter finally surrendered, and the Yukon's ice began to break up and move.

It began subtly as a hoarse, low rumble, at the same time near and extending far upstream. The intensity of the rumbles gradually increased until they became more like earthquake tremors. Birds suspended their singing and squirrels stopped chattering. Men stood in reverent awe of the powerful forces of river and ice. Grinding and groaning, the ice began to slip downstream, jamming again almost as soon as it moved. Once the big cakes of ice began to move, they scoured the islands and caromed against the banks of the Yukon, gouging out chunks of earth. London described this phenomenon in <u>A Daughter of the Snows</u>:

> A great cake had driven its nose into the bed of the river thirty feet below and was struggling to up-end. All the frigid flood behind crinkled and bent back like so much paper. Then the stalled cake turned completely over and thrust its muddy nose skyward. But the squeeze caught it, while cake mounted cake at its back, and its fifty feet of muck and gouge were hurled into the air. It crashed upon the moving mass beneath, and flying fragments landed at the feet of those that watched. Caught broadside in a chaos of pressures, it crumbled into shattered pieces and disappeared.[2]

The Yukon River served as a major highway for nearly all Klondike gold-seekers, whether following an all-water route or a route which included travel by land as well as by water. Jack London traveled into the Klondike during the summer and fall of 1897, following a land route over the Chilkoot Pass that led to the headwaters of the Yukon. At the same time, about eighteen hundred would-be Klondikers followed an all-water route, the last great leg of which was the mighty Yukon River. Less than fifty of those 1,800 gold-seekers reached Dawson before the river froze. The remaining 1,750 travelers were literally frozen in place, forced to hold up until the spring thaw, caught along the Yukon somewhere between the Bering Sea and the heart of the gold rush area.[3] These immobilized fortune-seekers were anxiously awaiting the breakup of the ice on the Yukon River.

Jack and his fellow miners on Split-Up Island were also waiting for the ice in the river to begin moving. They had suffered the scant hours of daylight throughout the dark, cold months. Now, as if a reward for their patience and perseverance, the hours of daylight increased each day, the sun began to linger in the sky, and the daily hours of darkness dwindled. The daylight temperatures began to be pleasant enough that a man could remove his coat outdoors and still be comfortable.

While waiting for the thaw to clear the river, Jack and Doc Harvey had kept themselves very busy tearing down their cabin, using its lumber to build a raft. This type of labor would have normally been easy for Jack when he was healthy, but it was slow and tedious because of his advanced case of scurvy.

By the time the river had thawed enough to become navigable, Doc Harvey and Jack were ready to set out for Dawson. They were anxious to leave immediately, before subsequent batches of ice-cakes came clamoring down from further upriver. Despite being sick, Jack took the tiller.

Doc Harvey and Jack's trip to Dawson was uneventful, except for one incident which Doc loved to relate for years to come.

The pair had learned that wood was fetching a high price in Dawson. Logs were preferred because they could be taken to the lumber mill and sold for a substantial bulk price. Even driftwood and scraps in any condition could be sold for firewood. So, when Doc and Jack pushed away from Split-Up Island, attached to their raft by a long length of rope was a big pile of driftwood the two had collected. This pile grew impressively as they traveled downriver, regularly adding to its bulk with especially choice pieces of wood they found along the way. The raft became unwieldy because of its growing, clumsy trailer of driftwood.

Once, when the raft became stuck on a bar and the big sweep they had painstakingly fashioned cracked as Jack leaned hard against it, his frustration erupted. "Doctor," he proclaimed with obvious disgust, "I don't know who made this world, but I believe I could make a damn sight better one myself!" From that day forward, Doc Harvey never tired of repeating the story and loved to refer to Jack's assessment of the world as "the most blasphemous thing I ever heard".[4]

It was late in May when Doc Harvey and Jack beached their raft near the sawmill at Dawson. They also successfully landed their huge, floating pile of driftwood. All of the logs from the raft and pile were sold to the mill for six hundred dollars. The new arrivals then sold the remaining scraps around Dawson for a few more dollars. Their resourcefulness and ambition had paid off well.

For Jack, the wood shortage in Dawson was a fortunate circumstance. Stricken with scurvy and facing impending medical costs, his share of the profits from the sale of the wood gave Jack the money he desperately needed to treat his illness. He was in very bad condition. His scurvy was crippling his already-swollen limbs. He had to get help immediately.

The hub of the Klondike Gold Rush was packed and teeming that spring of 1898.

When Jack arrived, Dawson was awash in especially high spring floodwaters. Its streets had become mostly boatways. The first floor of practically every building was flooded, and people lived "nonchalantly" from the second floor up to the rooftops. The high ground surrounding the town was covered with shacks, tents, and makeshift camps. The local Indians told stories of former floods that had been far worse, as when the waterline had reached halfway up Moosehide Mountain.

Luckily for Jack — and many other sick or injured Klondikers — a Jesuit missionary named William Judge had been in the Klondike for over a dozen years. Affectionately known as "The Saint of Dawson", Judge had arrived in Dawson early in the gold rush, when it was only a canvas and log village. He immediately began the establishment of a church and a hospital, both of which were named Saint Mary's.

Father Judge served as his own architect and contractor. The two new buildings gave this city at the heart of the gold rush a much-needed sense of civilization. Because of his selfless devotion to others, the Father became a symbol of Christian conscience in the wild and woolly gold rush town.

When the church was destroyed by a fire, those townsfolk who most appreciated his civilizing influence rallied around Father Judge. Enough donations were collected to build an even bigger church. An additional $35,000 was later raised to fund the completion of Saint Mary's Hospital. Jack's first days in Dawson were spent at this same hospital in May of 1898.[5]

In fact, Saint Mary's Hospital was the sole medical facility for the entire Klondike region. Droves of Klondikers appeared every week at its doors with a plethora of injuries and diseases. The majority of the sick suffered from scurvy at various stages.

The attentions of the legendary Father Judge and his overwhelmed staff saved many lives, including Jack London's. Jack was suffering miserably when he arrived in Dawson but quickly improved with the care he received at Saint Mary's. However, the priest soon informed his patient that he had done all that he could under the circumstances. He advised Jack to get back to civilization as soon as he possibly could so that he would have the best chance to recover without any lasting effects.

Jack was certainly not lonely while he was a patient in Dawson's only hospital. All of his local friends came to visit him practically every day, and some of them turned up several times a day.

After a few days, Jack was discharged from Saint Mary's and went to stay in Emil Jensen's tent. Jack lived there with Emil, Doc Harvey, Bert Hargrave, and Charlie Borg. The Bond brothers' cabin was nearby. Jack was very fortunate to have such good friends to stay with since the cheapest available room for rent in town cost one hundred dollars per month.

Despite his lingering case of scurvy, Jack made several

The Bond Brothers' cabin in Dawson City.
"Buck" in *The Call of the Wild* was based on their dog.

new friends during his short stay in Dawson. One of the more colorful people Jack met was a hootchie-kootchie dancer named Freda Moloof. Jack admired her dancing, recognized her "plucky spirit", and enjoyed many quip-filled conversations with the witty "Turkish Whirlwind Danseuse".

Apparently Freda was too "hot" for Dawson since later that year the Mounties closed her act down. The constabulary firmly believed that her version of "Little Egypt"-style dancing was "too inflammatory for the citizenry".[6] [This seems somewhat hypocritical in a town where the truly outrageous Diamond Tooth Gertie would be applauded within the next few years.]

Underscoring the generally desperate nature of the place, in the spring of 1898, anything for sale in Dawson was wildly expensive, especially food. Two hundred dozen eggs brought over the snows via Chilkoot Pass by dog sled just before the breakup of ice on the river were sold for $3,600; that is eighteen dollars a dozen at a time when the same number of eggs could be purchased in Seattle [1,350 miles south] for twenty-five cents. Because of the hunger for news, grease-streaked, month-old newspapers which originally sold for five to ten cents each were resold in Dawson for fifteen dollars apiece. It was rumored that a man reading a newspaper out loud could charge each listener a fee.

As soon as his condition improved, Jack went looking for work. He searched for any small job he could get, but the best way he found to make money was by picking up driftwood logs with a rowboat and towing them back to the mill "where they brought a fabulous price". Salvaging wood in this manner, Jack earned better than a miner's average wage of fifteen dollars a day.[7] London may have made additional money by collecting firewood from the hills behind Dawson.

However, Father Judge's limited treatments for his scurvy had not been enough for London to completely recover. His physical exertions to earn money coupled with his shaky bodily health, together with the shortage of fresh fruits and vegetables, threatened to contribute to a worsening of his condition, with the looming danger of a serious relapse . . . one which could be fatal. This underscored Jack's decision to take Father Judge's advice and leave Dawson as soon as he could.

On Tuesday, June seventh, Jack London, Charles Taylor, and John Thorson left Dawson in an open rowboat. Their destination was St. Michael on the coast of the Bering Sea. Their two-thousand mile journey would include eighty miles of sea coast.[8]

About that same date, Casswell Prewitt wrote to his family explaining that he had given up his place in a departing boat so that a very sick man could get out of the country.[9] That "very sick man" was Jack London, desperately attempting to quickly return to civilization.

Sailing downriver was the only real option for Jack in his handicapped condition. The other main route out of the Klondike was up the Yukon River and then over either White Pass or Chilkoot Pass. If Jack had waited two weeks longer, he could have booked passage for one hundred and fifty dollars on a rivergoing passenger steamer leaving Dawson and traveling to the mouth of the Yukon River.

But, why should Jack have waited and hustled for passage on the steamer when he was a very experienced small-boat sailor? Navigating the river and the coast to St. Michael was the least expensive and most reasonable way to leave. Even more importantly, with Jack's precarious condition, it was not advisable that he should tarry for even a single day.

Before he left, Jack acquired a small notebook to use as a diary, like the ones he had used "on the Road" in 1894 when he had tramped as "Sailor Kid" across the United States and Canada. In the notebook, he chronicled their progress downriver as well as recorded his thoughts and impressions. Much of what we know about Jack's trip out of the Klondike comes from this diary.[10]

Just before leaving Dawson, Jack and his traveling companions also talked with many "sailor and miner" friends. They heard quite a few "parting injunctions" and were given the honorable responsibility of passing on "love and business messages" to others downriver; "see so and so, & such a one," Jack wryly noted. Most of the friends who had a few last words with the trio expressed a sincere envy of those getting out of the Klondike, openly regretting their own decision to stay. In fact, most gold-seekers who were Jack's contemporaries in the Klondike would be out of the country in less than two years.

As Jack and his two companions in the boat pushed away from the shore, "Our friends attempted a half-hearted cheer, and filled the air with messages for those at home".[11]

Altogether, Jack London had spent about three and a half weeks in Dawson that spring.

When Jack left Dawson, the high water of the spring flood was receding, and in its place, great quagmires appeared. Any street in Dawson which was not underwater became instead a gelatinous morass that would challenge the fortitude of anyone who ventured to cross it. Dawson's main street was "a sea of mud, with men and horses floundering together in the sticky ditch, like sinners in the slimy pockets of Dante's hell".[12] London's handwritten last impression of the city was: ". . . dreary, desolate Dawson, built in a swamp, flooded to the second story, populated by dogs, mosquitoes and gold-seekers".[13]

"Dawson slowly fading away," Jack wrote in his notebook as they drifted downriver. He was "glad to get out of the jerry-built town where men sometimes went for their mail in canoes; where bartenders watered down bad whiskey to a third of its strength and restaurant owners charged five dollars for a poor meal; where fleas and floozies vied with each other for the miners' attention; where there was no piped water and no sewer; and where dozens of new buildings were springing up in the mud to take care of the suckers moving down from the passes and lakes and up from Seattle and St. Michael".[14]

After shoving off, London, Taylor, and Thorson drifted downstream effortlessly. The current ran steady and deliberate at about six miles an hour. The ice that had clogged the river just one month earlier had completely vanished.

The boat was rough-hewn; Jack would later describe it as "homemade, weak-kneed, and leaky".[15] In fact, the "small" craft was never given a name, and its exact dimensions remain unknown.

The three men in the small boat had brought only the necessary equipment: ample supplies, money to purchase food along the river and a steamship ticket to Seattle, leftovers from their outfits, souvenirs from their ordeals, and an old-fashioned, muzzle-loading, double-barreled shotgun. Jack declared in his notebook that the gun was not only old but also unpredictable. It consistently misfired. When the weapon did go off, one of the two triggers would *sometimes* fire both barrels.

Aside from bailing water and other necessary tasks, the trio decided that the mood of the voyage should be leisurely. They agreed that they had done enough work, trying to be prospectors and miners. They would take a vacation as they drifted downriver and let the current do most of the work. Jack wrote: "The three of us had sworn to make of this a pleasure trip, in which all labor was to be performed by gravitation, and all profit reaped by ourselves. And what a profit it was to us who had been accustomed to pack great loads on our backs or drag all day at the sleds for a paltry 25 or 30 miles".[16]

They left Dawson at four o'clock in the afternoon. They were unconcerned about the late afternoon departure since the "midnight sun" of the Northland summer was stretching the hours of daylight. Darkness was relegated to a brief period of less than an hour around midnight. Consequently, it was still not dark when they made their first stop at ten o'clock that evening.

Only seven miles downriver from Dawson, they passed the site of Fort Reliance, the former headquarters of the Alaska Commercial Company and the center of civilization in the area before the gold rush began in 1896.[17] In fact, Miner Bruce's map (which Jack carried) showed Fort Reliance — and not Dawson — since the map had been drawn in 1895, before Dawson existed. By the time Jack passed the site of Fort Reliance, the tables had turned completely: Dawson was now the central hub for the area, and Fort Reliance was little more than a ghost town.

After just a few hours in the boat, the three men determined that they could reach St. Michael much sooner if they made the boat suitable for round-the-clock travel. So, they pulled ashore, set up camp, and built a warm, roaring fire to mitigate the chill of the cold, steady drizzle that fell as they worked on their boat. After a few minor improvements, they sailed on to an Indian camp at 12-Mile Creek.[18]

They reached the camp at two in the morning. In keeping with their casual approach to the voyage, they decided to get some sleep.

After a good rest, they finished remodeling the rowboat. They arranged areas for a living room, a kitchen, and a bedroom on the boat. The bow was piled with firewood and, depending on the size of the pile, it sometimes served as another place to sit or lounge on the boat, or as Jack referred to it, the "living room".

Springy pine boughs were placed in the bottom at the middle of the boat to serve as a mattress for a "bunk". This bunk was covered with blankets and intended to accommodate two people. This was very important as it would allow them to drift downstream twenty-four hours a day while sleeping in rotating shifts. As long as one man was at the tiller, they could continue to sail safely forward.

A rower's bench, built two-thirds of the way back from the bow, separated the "bedroom" and the kitchen. This rower's bench was large enough to accommodate more than one man.

Their "snug little kitchen" was immediately after the rower's bench. This cramped but essential kitchen was designated by a Klondike (or Yukon) stove at its center. These stoves could be found on almost every small boat on the river. Directly behind the kitchen, crammed into the stern, was where the steersman would sit at the tiller. The entire affair was optimistically covered over with a fine-meshed netting intended to keep out mosquitoes.[19]

At eleven in the morning on Wednesday, June eighth, the boat was ready for continuous sailing. "It was a veritable home," London wrote, "and we had little need of going ashore, save out of curiosity or to lay in a fresh supply of firewood".[20] They pushed off into the chocolate-colored flow of the ice-freed Yukon and continued to drift toward the sea.

At three o'clock that afternoon, Jack and his companions reached Fortymile, so named for its distance from old Fort Reliance. The place was practically deserted, but those who remained informed them that they had been passed in the night — presumably while they all slept ashore — by the *May West*, a small river steamer, headed for Dawson with a six-ton cargo of whiskey. Jack's wry comment in his diary reads: ". . . hot time in Dawson as a consequence".

Not many miles downriver from Fortymile, they found Fort Cudahy "likewise deserted". As tourists in a ghost town, they briefly visited the bare-shelved store and the barracks devoid of troops before getting back in their rowboat to continue the journey.

Despite their pledge to do as little as possible, there were still some essential things that had to be done during their journey. Shortly after midnight on June ninth, they discussed the "arrangement of watches".

Since they were sailing twenty-four hours a day, someone always needed to be at the tiller, watching out for where they were going and keeping the boat out of trouble. They decided that two men could rotate in twelve-hour shifts at the tiller, with the third relieving or assisting the man on watch as needed. The third man could also cook meals. Jack and John Thorson took the "watches". Charley Taylor wanted to keep regular hours and sleep undisturbed through the night; accordingly, it was decided that he would be the boat's cook.

Jack took the first watch of midnight to noon, the first half of June ninth. He knew the hours of this watch would suit his temperament. His partners slept as he quietly guided their craft through the elongated twilight of the subarctic summer night. He would have many hours at the tiller to privately think and dream.

They were often not alone on the river. In fact, they were at the very beginning of a steady, month's-long, downriver migration by hundreds of other small boats. Like Jack, John, and Charley, many other men were drifting out of the Klondike on the Yukon River. In fact, Jeremiah Lynch, who started up the Yukon from its mouth a month later, counted one hundred and eleven such boats going downstream in a single day. The men on the boats would call to Lynch discouraging phrases such as, "Bad news . . . Cold winter . . . Poor grub . . . No work . . . Hundreds starving . . . Go Back!"[21]

Lynch and the incoming prospectors were part of what would become known as the third and final stage of the great Klondike Gold Rush. This stage continued over the next two years and included those who came too late to discover or to lay claim to rich gold deposits. To be sure, small finds were made, but nothing that would rival the discoveries made during the first and second stages of this gold rush.

As they sailed downstream, Jack and his friends passed an incoming flood of eager gold-seekers rushing upriver to Dawson. Steam-driven riverboats (also known as "steamers"), sailboats, rowboats, rafts, and canoes could be seen going both upstream and down along the arterial Yukon. The population of Dawson that summer would swell to about ten thousand.[22]

Many of the steamers were modern ships owned by the large trading companies. Others were floating antiques. One was the *W. K. Merwin* which had been towed by tug from Seattle to St. Michael and was described as "a seventeen-year-old stern-wheeler" which "looked like Noah's ark". The ship's unfortunate passengers had spent the winter near an Eskimo village in the Yukon River's delta because the *Merwin* had been caught as the river iced over. Other steamers included the diminutive *May West*, the first riverboat to reach Dawson [with the previously-mentioned cargo of whiskey], and the *Seattle No. 1*, scornfully nicknamed "The Mukluk" [after Eskimo footwear] because of its ugly appearance. The last two ships mentioned had been built the previous fall by "stranded argonauts" on the coast near St. Michael.[23]

Nine miles upriver from Eagle City, at two o'clock in the morning, Jack noted in his journal his sighting of the Alaska Commercial Company steamer *Victoria*. He observed that she was so fully loaded with hardware that there were "no passengers possible".

An hour and a half later, at three-thirty in the morning, they reached Eagle City.

The town was just across the Alaskan-Canadian border. Jack gleefully noted that he was "once again in Uncle Sam's dominions" since this was the first town on the American side of the boundary. He found about fifty townsfolk "engaged in a bucking faro layout". Gambling helped pass the time while these local folks waited for a steamer to arrive, bringing the first incoming food shipment since winter. Some were also waiting to book passage to Dawson.

Several players interrupted their spirited game in an attempt to sell "corner lots" to Jack and his traveling companions.[24] These plots were in-town real estate lots, supposedly on the corners at street intersections. But, Eagle City did not have that many corner lots, and the few that could be recognized were far from impressive. Jack and his companions were not fools and did not buy.

The trio left the game, got back in their boat, and continued downstream on the dependably "stiff", steady current. They navigated around the few islands they encountered as the river wound its way through the rugged, "sternly outlined" mountains.

At nine that morning, they spotted a moose swimming in the river to get away from the mosquitoes. Seizing on the chance to obtain some fresh meat, the three men sprang into action. Jack snatched up the ax and began shouting advice and directions. John Thorson gripped the oars and mightily rowed toward the moose. Charley Taylor took up the shotgun, already loaded with birdshot, and moved to the bow of the boat, where he stood ready to shoot.

As they rapidly closed in on the moose, Taylor prematurely

took aim and fired from too great a distance to be effective. The birdshot and the blast terrified the moose, which hastily swam to shore and madly stampeded off through the woods. The boat landed just a moment after the moose. Charley jumped out and ran after the animal. Jack and John were instantly swarmed with mosquitoes. They immediately started the smudge pots.

A few minutes later Charley reappeared, huffing and puffing with exertion, furiously cursing the moose and so thoroughly bitten by mosquitoes that it took him several days to recover. This was to be their only attempt to hunt for red meat on the trip.[25]

At four that afternoon, they passed another [unidentified] river steamer.

At ten o'clock that evening, they were hailed by a man along the shore. They hospitably picked him up and agreed to take him as a passenger as far as Circle City, not many miles downriver.

At 6:30 in the morning on June tenth, they passed another river steamer, the *Mayor Woods*, "high and dry on a bar with 170 passengers". This steamer had started upriver for Dawson the previous fall. Like the *Merwin*, it had been caught in the freeze, one hundred miles below Minook. With the thaw, the *Mayor Woods* had resumed its journey, only to run aground on the bar.

On the day Jack and his party floated by, they were hailed by some of the discouraged passengers who were seeking transportation back to St. Michael, even in a rowboat like the one Jack and his friends were using. But, Jack's small boat already seemed crowded by its one extra passenger.

Continuing on, they reached Circle City at about 8:30 that evening. They dropped off their passenger and went shopping for supplies, only to find a repeat of what they had seen at Fortymile: bare shelves, "no sugar, butter nor milk". All three men enjoyed smoking and, as some consolation, they did manage to find some tobacco for sale. Jack also wrote in his notebook that the mosquitoes were making a "demonstration in force".

Circle City was just inside a huge, sprawling swampland known as the Yukon Flats. This vast and "dismal domain" extended for about fifty miles to the east, one hundred miles to the north, and well over one hundred miles to the west. Nine rivers joined the Yukon on its winding course through "the Flats".

In June of 1898, the spring floodwaters were exceptionally high. In the Flats, the Yukon and its tributary rivers spread over and divided around "thousands of millions" of islands. In many cases, the islands had been or still were flooded, leaving the air dank and humid. The once-strong current of the Yukon diffused and slowed as the main channel divided around the multiple islands and into proliferating channels. Forever lost in its journey to the sea, driftwood collected in immense piles everywhere. Wildlife was abundant, especially waterfowl such as geese.

"One finds himself in a gigantic puzzle," London wrote of it later, "consisting of thousands of miles of territory, and cut up into countless myriads of islands and channels".[26]

Saturday, June eleventh, was a typical summer's day in the land of the midnight sun. Having lived through the sub-zero winter, they now found themselves "sweltering in a tropical temperature under Arctic Skies".[27] By noon, the heat was intense, and the humidity was extremely high.

Jack did not fail to recognize this astonishing range of seasonal temperatures. Only a month before, he could have frozen to death in broad daylight, but by June, it was consistently warm, even at midnight. The danger of freezing to death lingered only high in the mountains, out on the glaciers, or on the vast northern ice fields. Sunset, twilight, night, morning twilight, and sunrise all took place in approximately one hour with the darkness or "no sun" phase lasting only half that long (from 11:45 P.M. until 12:15 A.M., according to Jack London's notes). With each new dawn, the sun reappeared for the rest of the day until 11:45 that evening.

At this stage of their journey, life on the boat had settled into a comfortable routine. As Jack later wrote, "We now hunted, played cards, smoked, ate and slept, sure of our six miles an hour, of our 144 a day".[28]

After leaving Circle City, the original trio never picked up another human passenger on their journey to St. Michael despite being hailed almost daily by men stranded in boats or along the shore. Chances are that the brief time they had the fourth man on board convinced them that three was enough.

They crossed the Arctic Circle at three in the morning and arrived at Fort Yukon one hour later. Founded in 1847, this was the first English-speaking settlement in the Yukon. Its economy was originally based on the British colonial fur trade's ability to compete with the Russians. Jack and his two companions watched as Indians and Klondikers energetically transferred goods out of a nearby cache and onto the steam-powered riverboat *Bella*. London later described what he had witnessed at Fort Yukon in "From Dawson to the Sea":

> It was a peculiar scene of animation and excitement. Four o'clock in the morning, under the Arctic Circle, yet the sun was high in the heavens and it was already uncomfortably warm. It seemed more like some festival day at 3 o'clock in the afternoon. All was gaiety, noise and laughter. The bucks were skylarking or flirting with the maidens; the older squaws were gossiping in bunches, while the young ones shrank and giggled in the corners. The children played or squabbled, and the babies rolled in the muck with the tawny wolf-dogs. Fantastic forms, dimly outlined, flitted to and fro, surged together, eddied, parted, in the smoke-laden atmosphere. Only by nosing and poking about could one see anything; for the reeking smoke rose from untold smudges, bringing grief to the mosquito, tears to the soft eyes of the white men and giving to the whole affair a mysterious air of unreality.

The gaiety of this loading party was significant. During the winter, when residents of Dawson and many of the surrounding camps had been on the verge of starvation, Fort Yukon's caches had been filled to overflowing with vital supplies, mostly food. Once the river had frozen, all navigation had utterly ceased, and these supplies could not be distributed and had remained at the Fort. To attempt to transport the supplies over the 250 miles of rugged terrain and deep snow to Dawson would have taken two or three weeks and was considered too dangerous. So, the men on the riverboat were in high spirits because they realized that the provisions they were loading would finally reach those hungry souls upriver who had suffered through the winter with very limited supplies.[29]

Jack and his traveling partners left Fort Yukon and resumed their journey. Several hours downriver, at nine o'clock, they passed the steamer *Hamilton* and came to the junction of the Yukon and Porcupine Rivers, which looked more like a mile-wide bay. Several nearby rivers also fed into the Yukon River at this juncture. Here the flow of the mighty Yukon made a ninety-degree turn in direction from northwest to southwest. With this huge sweeping turn, the swollen river grew wider and began to resemble a lake with most of its shoreline diverging into the Flats. London would later appropriately describe this area as a "lasuctrine wilderness". The river then continued its journey across the breadth of Alaska.

At Dawson, the Yukon River had been a mile wide at the bend. The river had grown to a width of eight miles by the time they had reached Fort Yukon. Before their journey was over, London and his companions would see the swollen river sprawl as wide as forty miles [at Anvik].

As they drifted along through the sodden realm of the Flats, the mountains receded, becoming a distant horizon beyond the ocean of reeds and scrub brush which now surrounded them. They noticed scattered Indian camps and many deserted cabins. Jack observed that many of the Indians in this area were physically larger and more muscular than most of the Northern natives he had seen. He described them as "big husky fellows" and observed they were often employed by white men as "woodchoppers, deck hands, etc.". He also noted that a river pilot working on the Yukon that summer could expect to be paid five dollars a day.

In the Flats, clouds of mosquitoes hung everywhere over the swampy land and the water. The three men in their small, open boat were constantly under attack. Their main defense against the voracious blood-sucking insects was their "mosquito rig" which consisted of framing poles hung with fine-meshed nets creating a protected enclosure. Their second line of defense was the smoke from the smudge pots which the trio kept constantly burning "on every hand". Truly effective mosquito repellants had not yet been developed, and the ointments recommended for that purpose during Jack's time were often as obnoxious as the pests.

Jack must have begun to realize that writing was one possible way in which he might be able to salvage some of the time he had spent and some of the expenses he had incurred while seeking his fortune in the Klondike. Surely, his firsthand observations and experiences would be of interest to the newspapers and magazines worldwide which had sent their reporters to and printed accounts of the "new El Dorado". As he jotted down notes in his diary, he was already thinking of writing a few nature study articles for juvenile journals; he mentioned two by name in his notes, "Outing" and "Youth's Companion".

That evening and night were strikingly gorgeous. Jack was so moved that he made notes of the sights and sounds. He later wrote this from his notes and memories:

> . . . And the strange beauty and charm of the noonday nights — drifting, always drifting with the stream. Now slipping down a narrow channel where the wooded shores seem to meet overhead; now flashing into the open, where a thousand streams converge and form a mighty river; and again the diverging courses, the tiny channel, the overhanging forest, the smell of the land and the damp warmth of the vegetation. And above all, the hum of life, bursting into sudden gushes of song, slowly swelling to a great, dull roar of satisfaction or dying away into sweetly cadenced silence. Not a sound as we round the tail of a bar, disturbing a solitary crane from his ghostly reveries. A partridge drums in the forest, a moose lunges noisily as it takes to the water, and again silence. Then an owl hoots from some gloomy recess or a raven croaks gutturally overhead. Suddenly, the wild cry of a loon sweeps across a glassy stretch of river, awakening myriad answers. The robins open their full, rich throats and the woods burst into music. The tree squirrels play half a dozen instruments at once, while the blackbirds sing shrill choruses to the sharp-marked time of the woodpecker. The pure treble of the songbirds is accompanied by the steady boom boom of the partridge, till all is lost in the general pandemonium. Then the wild fowl of the swamp join the quick crescendo, and the finale, swelled to bursting, slowly dies away. A kildee calls timidly to its mate, and silence falls.[30]

On the twelfth, the three men in their rowboat slowly drifted along through the watery maze. It was a leisurely day except for the vital need to stay in the main channel as much as possible. A mistake in judgment — taking a wrong channel — could result in straying into a labyrinth of subsequent channels, some dead-ends. Days could be lost while attempting to rejoin the swampy region's principal outflow. The maps they had were not detailed and basically useless for navigating through the Flats. One way they had of staying in the main channel was to follow the direction of the current. Jack's sailing experience undoubtedly also helped. However, at times the water was so still that it seemed as though they were afloat on a lake, making it very difficult to follow the main channel. To make matters worse, the Flats had few landmarks which could be seen from a distance, and the reeds and scrub brush along the shores frequently obscured their view of the horizon.

Jack and his companions found some entertainment in occasionally shooting at geese. With the shooting came a natural preoccupation with the old muzzle-loading shotgun.

They succumbed to the boyish urge to experiment with bigger, more powerful loads of gunpowder and shot. They were using old-style, black gunpowder at about twice the required amount. Jack cryptically jotted in his diary, "Loaded 4½ drams, with 15 large buckshot; kicked John's arm". This was a potentially dangerous situation since overloaded guns can explode.

There were geese in countless numbers in the Flats. Their nests were especially plentiful along the shore. Despite his poor health, Jack zealously helped collect the abundant goose eggs. He gathered the eggs because, like many men in the Klondike at that time, Jack erroneously believed that fresh food, such as red meat and eggs, would improve his worsening scurvy.[31]

Mountains were again becoming visible as they followed the main channel to the far southwestern side of the Flats. The current was still sluggish and their progress was slow; but, at last, they could see that they were certainly moving out of the gigantic swamp. Not only were they now past the danger of getting lost in the maze-like Flats, but they also looked forward to some thinning of the huge clouds of mosquitoes once they returned to a properly-flowing river. As they drifted slowly that evening, every smudge pot was burning to discourage the multitude of hungry mosquitoes.

On the morning of June 13, Jack's party arrived at Fort Hamilton on the far western edge of the Yukon Flats, where the river came out of the swamplands. This was normally a "white man's" settlement, but a few days before Jack's arrival, every white man in the area had left for Dawson. Therefore, he saw only Indians at the Fort.

They continued downriver until noon, when they stopped at a coal mine above Minook. The two men "working it" were R. E. Russell of Seattle and an unnamed fellow from Toledo, Ohio. Jack wrote in his diary that the highwater of the summer flood had not only inundated the pair's mine but had also carried away their cabin and coal bunker. Nevertheless, the two spunky men had piled salvaged coal on high ground and sold it to passing steamers for $25 per ton. Of these two men, Jack noted empathetically: "Faces covered with clay, hard job fighting mosquitos. Bid them farewell amid clouds of the same personified ubiquity".

At four o'clock that afternoon, Jack and his traveling companions arrived at Minook. This was the principal gold mining town along the lower half of the river. The population of the settlement on that day was about five hundred people and, as usual, was primarily men.

As was true all along the river, everyone in Minook was hungry for any sort of news. Most of them had heard nothing from the "outside" since the beginning of the previous winter. As a result, Jack and his companions found themselves bombarded with inquiries. They found the folks they spoke to mostly "perturbed over the war, the Thanksgiving football game and the execution of Durant" [*sic*].[32] These phrases from Jack's diary reveal three of the most controversial, contemporary issues for Klondikers: the Spanish-American War (which had been fought between February and June), the rival football game between Stanford and the University of California at Berkeley (the biggest sporting event of the year in California, where many Klondikers were from), and the fate of the defendant [Durrant] in the intriguing "girl in the belfry" murder case [which occurred in San Francisco, California].[33]

Jack and his companions tried their best to satisfy the inhabitants of Minook's hunger for news of the outside world. "True to Northland tradition," he wrote, "we expanded items into chapters, yet failed utterly in satisfying their unholy lust for news".[34]

As luck would have it, the first man to greet Jack was an "old acquaintance" named Chestnut. Jack knew Chestnut from his days as a student at the University of California in Berkeley and referred to him in the diary as "a university man".

In Minook, Jack also met a Captain Mayo, who had been in the region for thirty years. Jack noted Mayo was a very pleasant conversationalist and was "getting stout".

When Jack and his companions were there, gold in Minook was selling for $18.75 per ounce. This was somewhat of a bargain since the price of an ounce of gold "in the states" at that time was $20.67. [A twenty-dollar United States gold coin minted at that same time contained slightly less than an ounce of pure gold.]

Jack matter-of-factly stated that the "Minook district will turn out $85,000" during "that period".[35] This gives us an idea of the volume of gold that was coming out of the area at that time.

During his several hours in Minook, Jack also learned that fraud was afoot. As he noted in his diary, "Some company faking a number of creeks here and selling stock on outside at $1.00 per share." He added that there were one million shares of the worthless stock available.

After leaving Minook, Jack and his fellow travelers drifted past the settlement of Rampart. At eleven o'clock that evening, they ran the quick series of rapids where the Yukon River passed through the Ray Mountains.

Even though it was brief, the rapids finally allowed the best relief yet from the mosquitoes. After the rapids, the general onslaught of mosquitoes continued, but it was not nearly as miserable as it had been in the Flats. On the open river, fewer mosquitoes swarmed at the center, so by staying as distant as possible from the shore, the travelers could minimize the mosquitoes they encountered. However, the moment they landed or even approached the shore, clouds of the voracious pests would immediately form around them.

In the first hours of Tuesday, June fourteenth, they came to the Tanana River junction. Jack's entry in his notebook revealed that they "stopped at Tanana Station just above St. James Mission & situated at the Indian town of Muklukyeto, at the junction of the Yukon & Toyikakat Rivers". According to Jack, the camp was "large". Many Indians had just come down the Tanana for the annual upstream run of the salmon which was just about to occur. The riverbanks were lined with the natives' birch-bark canoes. Fish nets were "in evidence everywhere", and everything was "ready for the fish".

Jack and his friends soon discovered that a dance was in progress. The party was taking place in a "large log structure" nearby.[36] They went to the cabin and jostled their way through the long, low interior. The smoke and heat were stifling.

The room presented a fascinating scene. The Indians wildly stepped and hooted to "white man's dances" in a full-flung melee.

Jack and his friends believed they were the only white men present and "prepared to enjoy the novelty of the situation . . . with the peculiar elation of the traveler who scales the virgin peak". But, they were disappointed when they spotted another white man across the crowded room. Jack reported they were "dizzy with the heat and the smell of bodies" when they "discerned the fair, bronzed skin, the blue eyes, the blond moustache of the ubiquitous Anglo-Saxon".[37]

London noticed that it was five o'clock in the morning and that the entire village was up celebrating. He tersely noted in his diary, "children playing, bucks skylarking; squaws giggling & flirting, dogs fighting, etc.", and then added, "Soon all will be asleep, for they sleep all day, and work and play at night".

Once the village had settled down for its daily rest, Jack and his companions re-hung their mosquito nets and quietly pushed their boat away from shore. They soon passed the old Saint James mission. They continued lazily drifting downstream for many long hours.

At midnight it became Wednesday, June 15. Jack began

his watch at the tiller. The mosquitoes were exceptionally thick. Before long, he began to faintly hear the distant chants of Indians ahead of them several miles downriver. The chanting grew gradually louder and, in a little more than an hour (at 1:30 A.M.), they landed at another Indian camp where a big pagan celebration was in progress.

"Climbing the bank," Jack wrote of it later, "we came full upon the weird scene. It brought us back to the orgies of the caveman and more closely in touch with our common ancestor . . . Several score of bucks were giving tongue to unwritten music, evidently born when the world was very young, and still apulse with the spirit of primeval man. Urged on by the chief medicine man, the women had abandoned themselves to the religious ecstacy, their raven hair unbound and falling to their hips, while their bodies were swaying and undulating to the swing of the song".[38]

They were somewhere near or at Kokrines, about 100 miles downriver from Tanana Station. Amid the singing bucks and dancing women, Jack noticed a particularly striking young woman. "Beautiful, half-breed woman," he wrote in his diary. "Caucasian features, slender form, delicate oval of face & head". He reminded himself to "describe her environment". His last recorded thought regarding the woman was: "How much harder her lot than the Japanese Half Caste".

At the village, they met another "ubiquitous Anglo-Saxon". By now, Jack had come to consider the Anglo-Saxons as being practically everywhere and "always at home in any environment". Jack described the nameless fellow at the village as a "White man from Sacramento" who was living with the Indians and chopping cords of wood to sell while waiting for the salmon run to reach their village on the river.

After spending a couple of hours at the camp, the three men climbed in their rowboat and once again shoved away from shore. At five-thirty that morning, they passed the steamer *Alice*, a heartwarming sight since rumors upriver had stated that the ship had been "lost in the ice" with no survivors. The *Alice* was immediately followed by the *Marguerite*, another river steamer.

Jack and his friends sailed the rest of the day with very

few distractions. "8 P. M. White man starting a store. Indian camps, etc." Jack wrote with an air of discernible boredom. At ten that evening, they stopped at another native village. Jack surveyed the scene and wrote the last entry of the day in his diary: "10 P. M. Indian village, only old people left. The perpetual cry for medicine. Stoicism of the sufferers. Traces of white blood among the papooses everywhere apparent".

After a very brief stop, they continued their downriver journey in the rowboat.

The next day was Thursday, June 16. At three in the afternoon, they reached a flooded North American Trading and Transportation Company station near the Koyokuk River junction. They had been drifting for hours through seemingly endless, swamplike stretches filled with colorful waterfowl and the ever-present clouds of mosquitoes. The people who had lived at the station were camped on nearby hillsides above the flood-heightened shoreline. Jack and his group bought some whitefish from them.

They also met a party of travelers preparing to follow the Koyokuk River through another vast swampland, continuing northward until they reached the river's headwaters in the Brooks Range [the major east-west mountain chain in northern Alaska]. There were predictions that the Alaskan Koyokuk headwaters region would yield gold in amounts similar to the Klondike.

Had his health been better, Jack may have joined this stampede, but his poor condition due to scurvy made that impossible. As it turned out, it was just as well for the big strike the group was hoping to find never materialized. Some gold would be found in that region, but nothing to rival the discovery that Carmack had made at Bonanza Creek.

As they continued downriver, Jack and his friends met several more such parties, all hoping to be the first to establish a gold-town like Dawson in the midst of the sprawling Brooks Range.

They reached Nulato at 9:30 that evening. This was known as the oldest settlement in the Yukon.[39] They were now about 650 miles from where the mouth of the Yukon River met the Bering Sea.

They decided to visit the Roman Catholic mission, and upon entrance, found themselves in the middle of a service.

As the congregation sang, the shrill voices of the chanting Indian women mixed with the low-toned voices of the men, creating what Jack described as a "weird effect". He also noticed that the Indians at Nulato had a healthier, better-dressed look than the natives he had seen at most other places on the river. He concluded in his diary that the Indians always looked better around the missions because of the missionaries' work and care.

After the service, the three travelling companions met Father Monroe, a delicately-featured, black-robed priest in moccasins. Jack discovered that the priest was a well-cultured Frenchman who had "devoted his life to his task". At the time the dedicated friar met Jack, he had already lived and worked zealously at the mission for five years.

By Friday, the seventeenth, they were back on the river. Two-thirds of their river odyssey was complete as they were now within seven hundred miles of St. Michael, the end of the Alaskan leg of their journey.

"Uneventful," Jack began his entry for that day. He then continued, making notes of the "evidences of the ice" and flood. They passed numerous and striking examples of the power of the ice as it traveled downriver. Huge chunks of earth had been ripped away by the ice-cakes and flood. Entire islands had been swept clear of trees. The floodwaters which had consistently surrounded them as they drifted toward the sea on the lower Yukon was, according to London's notes, the "greatest highwater known in many years, as a proof, flooding of old established towns, stations & native villages".

Commenting on the absence of geese, London added in his notebook, "but ducks becoming quite thick as we near the mouth". He also mentioned seeing Indian camps bristling with freshly-taken bear skins, stretched to dry in the sun. He described the unique-looking Indian graves he could see along the riverbank. He acknowledged the occasional "curiously carved totem pole". "Older graves more roughly made," he wrote, and parenthetically reminded himself of the palings [wooden pickets] used in the construction of shrines over the gravesites. He noted that the palings "shed the rain".

Regarding these Indian graves, Jack later commented:

"They have quite a reverence for their dead . . . their burial places being neat, clean and pleasing to the eye. Rough palings surround the graves, which are usually covered with a rain shed. Fantastic designs are often painted upon them by the means of soot and seal oil".[40]

Jack recognized the Catholic flavor of the monuments at most of the gravesites. He concluded that this was evidence of the relatively greater success of the Catholic, as opposed to the Protestant, missionary efforts. In his diary, Jack concluded that the "bare meetinghouse puritanical mode" of the Protestant service was no match for the "more impressive ritual" of the Catholic service, "so pregnant with mysticism". "But beyond a doubt," he finished, "much is due to the indefatigable efforts of the fathers".

"Sun rises like a ball of copper" Jack wrote in his notebook on Saturday, June 18. Commenting on the profusion of birds, he observed "woodpeckers, swallows, kingfishers, sea-gulls" and many others he "could not classify". He also took more notes regarding the damage from the ice that had come crashing down the river with the thaw only one month before. "Large trees uprooted or literally sawed in two by ice," he wrote. "Small trees tender bark stripped, and stand stretching their bleached limbs heavenward, mute witness to the Ice God's wrath".

During Jack's midnight watch, his companions snored under the mosquito nets while swarms of the pests attacked incessantly. One night after Jack had been bitten badly, John Thorson claimed he had watched two gangs of mosquitoes rush the netting, "one gang holding up the edge while a second gang crawled under". Not to be outdone by this tall tale, Charles Taylor swore that he had seen "several of the largest ones pull the mesh apart & let a small one squeeze through". Jack added to his notes detailing this bantering: "I have seen them with their proboscis bent and twisted after an assault on sheet iron stove." He also mentioned that the blood-thirsty bugs had bitten him through overalls *and* heavy underwear.

As they drifted downriver past villages and small settlements, Indians looking for trade paddled out to meet them mid-river. At one point, an abandoned malamute dog swam out to their rowboat. Seeing that the dog was tired and floundering, they brought it aboard. They discovered the animal had a broken leg and decided to keep it with them until they could find someone to care for it.

They reached Anvik at ten o'clock in the evening. The town was awash from the early summer flood. An Episcopal missionary pressed the trio to stay for "at least one Christian Sunday". Politely declining the offer, they pressed on to the trading company's local station where a man they happened to know, named Pickett, was in charge. Consequently, the three men were given a hearty welcome. More importantly, Jack received a can of tomatoes and some fresh potatoes.

Without having mentioned it previously in his diary, Jack wrote, ". . . my scurvy, which has now almost entirely crippled me from waist down. Right leg drawn up, can no longer straighten it, even in walking must put my whole weight on toes." This was a further indication that Jack had probably eaten no vitamin C-containing foods since Dawson.

Jack understood the seriousness of his situation. With clear-eyed whimsy, he reflected in his diary, "These few raw potatoes & tomatoes are worth more to me at the present stage of the game than an Eldorado claim — What wots it, though a man gain illimitable wealth & lose his own life?"

After finding someone who wanted the injured malamute dog, the trio prepared to leave Anvik. It had been a brief but important stop for Jack, especially in helping his scurvy. They continued downriver at 11:30 that same evening. Their next planned stop was Icogmute.

The swollen river was more like a large, moving lake taking them toward the sea. In his slightly improved condition, as he watched the low, distant hills recede and reappear on his right, Jack considered his future in "the land that listens . . . the land that broods".[41]

Despite getting lost in one of the numerous sloughs that branched out for miles in the flood, they managed to reach Holy Cross by the afternoon of June nineteenth. As they landed, the bucolic scene of grassy hills and the surrounding neatly-fenced farmlands made Jack feel a twinge of homesickness, undoubtedly made more poignant by his infirmity.

They learned that the Holy Cross Catholic Mission was headquarters for the Roman Catholic Church in Alaska, and that four Catholic sisters had recently been dispatched to assist Father Judge in Dawson. This must have been gratifying news for Jack who knew from firsthand experience how sorely their help was needed.

While at the Holy Cross Mission, Jack also chatted with a steward from the river steamer *Hamilton*.

Before leaving, Jack and his companions also traded with the Indians at Holy Cross for ducks, duck eggs, grouse, goose, and fish, but perhaps most importantly, for berries. Berries contain significant amounts of vitamin C and would certainly have helped to alleviate Jack's scurvy.

At one o'clock in the afternoon on Monday, June 20, Jack's party was forced by "bad weather" to put into shore for the rest of the day.

On June 21, they continued downstream, passing many Malamute [also "Malemute"] villages and stopping to visit at several. Jack was not very impressed by the Malamutes, whom he later defined as "a sort of mongrel cross of Thlinket and Esquimau [Eskimo]". He also described a typical Malamute dwelling as ". . . merely holes in the ground, shored with driftwood timbers", and added, "In the center of this they build an open fire, the smoke of which escapes from a venthole in the roof". Regarding their food, he commented: ". . . they continue to exist on a straight fish and meat diet, washed down with incalculable quantities of vile-smelling seal oil".[42]

Jack watched Malamute squaws making rope from bark. Stripping the bark from the roots of trees, they carefully slit the pieces into long, string-like strips. After wetting the strings, the squaws braided them together into a strong and flexible three-stranded rope. Jack noted that the women were responsible for "all such things, tanning leather, making nets, muc luc, mocassins" plus the added tasks of "weaving grass matting, minding dogs, papooses, etc. etc.".

They reached Icogmute at six o'clock that evening. This was the site of an early Russian mission, evidenced by the triple cross atop the church.[43] Consequently, the place was known (and may be found on maps today) as "Russian Mission" (not Icogmute). They traded a deck of cards for an Orthodox crucifix and met only one white man. He was a

Russian who, as London noted, "could not understand English". He was also the only surviving member of the Russian Orthodox missionary staff which had been assigned to that post. Aside from being flooded, Jack and his companions found Icogmute to be "very sleepy" and a "very miserable place".

Later that evening at an Indian village further downstream, they were able to trade two cups of flour for a king salmon [also known as chinook or spring salmon]. This fish was a welcome change in diet for men who had grown very weary of waterfowl eggs.[44]

For June 22, the entire inscription in Jack's diary reads: "Trading native villages. Nothing important".

Jack began his June 23 entries with, "Long stretches of flats". They were entering the Yukon Delta region. This country began with stretches of low, barren hills which were divided by large open fields and marshes. These alternating sections of hills and marshes gradually disappeared, giving way to miles of marshland extending as far as the eye could see. The river had etched short bluffs in the hills, defining the striking points of its turns. Malamute villages appeared frequently, practically lining the river.

At eleven that evening, they reached the Yukon's junction with the Andreasky River, where there was a flooded-out settlement of the same name. They traveled about two miles up the confluence of the main branch and "East Fork" of the tributary river to visit a large Indian village where most of the displaced residents from Andreasky were living. "How miserable their condition," Jack observed after watching the natives, but then commented, "yet how happy". He also noted how the natives would sit on the banks of the river, naked (or practically so) in the "chill north wind". These Indians were hoping to trade, sell curios, or exchange their fresh fish or game for flour with travelers passing by.

At midnight on Friday, June 24, Jack was struck by the sight of a Malamute Indian paddling his kayak across the water in the fleeting moonlight of the Alaskan summer night. The native's lyrical chant lilted across the water and complemented the idyllic scene. This prompted Jack to write "weird effect" in his notebook. In addition, he jotted a note about the local Indians: "They seem never to sleep, are always up". Following a few hours respite in the Indian village, they were back on the water.

After passing Andreasky and rejoining the flow of the Yukon, the low hills behind them shrank from view. Jack recorded, "And we entered the great Yukon Delta, for a 126 mile run to Kutlik". What he probably referred to here was the Pastol Bay village now known as Kotlik, about sixty miles southwest of St. Michael.

"Threading the maze" of the myriad of delta channels would not be easy. They had decided to avoid the expense of hiring a Malamute Indian guide despite being cognizant of the inconvenience and possible danger that getting lost in the marshland entailed. Instead of relying on an experienced local native, they decided to navigate the marshy labyrinth by themselves using a compass, several maps, and good common sense.

Soon after setting out on their own, Jack and his companions came upon an eerie setting — an entire fishing village, completely deserted.

"No signs of human life," London tersely noted.

They continued, then came upon another and another — villages devoid of Indians. There were no corpses or other evidence of catastrophe. It looked as though all of the natives had simply picked up and left. As they drifted by the empty villages, the three travelers must have speculated about what might have caused all the natives to leave.

They were now deep within the maze of the delta. They had not seen any white men since Tuesday when they had met the non-English-speaking Russian at Icogmute. They "threaded" the Yukon Delta "all day" and reached Aphorn Mouth, the beginning of the northernmost spur of the river which joins the sea at Kutlik.

On Saturday, June 25, they reached Hamilton Station, nearly halfway to Kutlik from where they had left the main branch of the Yukon. They learned that they must have passed the oceangoing steamer *John J. Healy*, which was said to be anchored at Andreasky. This was significant because they might have been able to sail south from Andreasky. They were also told that until the sixteenth of June [just nine days earlier], no oceangoing steamers had been able to reach St. Michael. And, they solved the mystery of the Indians missing from the deserted villages they had discovered the day before: the Indians were hunting seal "in the south channel", as the season dictated.

Eight miles further along the channel brought them to Bill Moore's place. According to Jack, Bill Moore was a man who had completely lost his ambition. Jack observed in his diary that the "hurry-scurry devil take the hindmost competition of civilization has no attraction" for Moore. Bill was a "squaw man" (a white man with an Indian wife) who had settled down in the marshes of the Yukon River Delta, building a dock and a house, which also served as a trading post. Jack noted that the Indians were proud to call Bill "brother-in-law" but somberly observed "how bleak and blank his existence".[45]

That evening, they reached Kutlik. It was Jack's "first smack of old ocean"; it had been almost a year since he had packed up the Dyea River to Chilkoot Pass. They camped along the banks of the river mouth that evening with the "open sea in sight". Despite their relative inexperience and lack of a local Indian guide, they had successfully crossed 120 miles of the Yukon River Delta on their own in only two days.

The next day was Sunday, June 26. They were about fifty miles southwest of St. Michael, where they expected to find an oceangoing steamship to take them south. Jack rigged a canvas sail. Once they were underway, he followed the shoreline just outside of the breakers. After sailing about twenty-five miles that day, they camped on a beach within sight of Point Romanoff.

On Monday, the weather was windy and the water was rough. Soon after shoving off, they were surprised to see a three-hatched kayak precariously crashing through the surf nearby and obviously in trouble. In the highest tradition of seamanship, Jack came alongside the wildly bobbing craft as his partners plucked off the only person aboard. They then tied a rope to the kayak and let it follow behind them.

The man they had picked up was Father Aloysius J. Robaut, one of the more active Jesuit missionaries in the area at that time. [London wrote the name as "Roubeau" in his diary.] Although Jack's party had no way of knowing it, this friar's reputation in Alaska was virtually legendary.

Father Robaut explained that he was also going to St. Michael and was "having a hard time in the surf".[46] The three men in the skiff offered to give him a lift up the coast while towing his kayak behind them. The missionary accepted their offer, then sat down next to Jack at the tiller.

One of the first things that occurred after the missionary came aboard was an "argument" over what day it was — Sunday or Monday. [It was Monday.]

Jack could not help but admire Robaut's utilitarian sense of style. The scurvy-sickened young writer scribbled in his diary later that day, recording his impressions of the interesting man he had met: "Dress — fur cap, coarse blue shirt, muc luc sea boots . . . how unlike a father on first sight". Jack asked if Robaut would object to him smoking. "On the contrary," the friar responded and indicated his pipe was "in the bidarka" [the Russian word for kayak].

So, cigarettes were rolled and pipes were pulled out in the small, crowded boat. As all four men enjoyed a smoke, the missionary spoke of himself and his work. Personable and chatty, the father casually admitted that he was "possessed of fatal faculty of getting lost". This would prove to be a haunting admission.

"He was an illustration of the many strange types to be found in the Northland," Jack wrote of Robaut later. "And for all the cloth, he was a jolly fellow, pulling an oar, smoking a pipe, or telling a tale with the next one".[47]

While talking to him, London learned that Robaut had been born to Italian parents in the southeastern seaport town of Nice, France. He had been educated and taken the vows of a Jesuit priest ["obedience, poverty, chastity"] in Spain. However, the friar now considered himself to be an American by residence and had been a missionary in Alaska for more than twelve years.

The father was "quite a linguist", capable of speaking fluent English (as with Jack and his companions), French, Italian, and Spanish. He had also learned the major Indian languages of the region as well as many of the dialects. Using his knowledge of languages, Robaut had worked out a system of grammar for the Innuit language and considered that accomplishment the "pride of his life".

In the afternoon, the travelers beached their boat, camping and resting until late that evening.

At eleven o'clock that evening, they "turned out", dismantled camp, and loaded their boat. The weather was still windy, and the Bering Sea was even choppier than the day before. It proved to be "quite a task" when they tried to run the boat through the breaking surf at the shoreline, especially with the kayak in tow. However, once they succeeded in getting out past the breakers, Jack's skills as a small-boat sailor kept them afloat and on course.

At midnight it became Tuesday, June twenty-eighth. A southeast wind brought intermittent squalls that energetically blasted rain in their faces. As they made their way up the coastline, the weather grew gradually worse. The sky to the south grew darker and the temperature dropped. The rain became more frequent.

Except for the responsibility of his passengers, Jack reveled in the challenge of sailing the turbulent sea. He shortened the boat's sail "to storm canvas" and ran before the fury of the wind. The unoccupied kayak in tow followed behind them, tethered to the rope and performing "strange feats", alternatively airborne or plunging and rolling in the surf as the "big seas" came "tumbling after".

In the midst of the storm they came upon the opening to a canal which Father Robaut believed followed the coastline for several miles inland and then would return them to the sea. By taking the canal, they could avoid the choppy waters on the coast.

Jack expertly shifted the sail from one side of the boat to the other ("jibe over"), and they whizzed past a boat at anchor in the mouth of the canal. The men on the other boat laughed because they believed that the canal was a dead end.

Oblivious to the other sailors' discouragement, the little rowboat sailed confidently by, continuing inland with the kayak in tow and disappearing up the canal. After some time had passed, the rowboat did not return. Doubting their own information, the men in the other boat changed their minds, pulled up anchor, and followed Jack's party. But, Robaut had made a mistake, and both boats ended up lost in a maze of canals and channels. While they were lost, Father Robaut helped as he could, "at an oar or on the towline". Finally, after seven hours of being lost in the coastal marshlands, they found the right canal. Jack complained in his diary that mistakes of navigation were very easy to make in the canals of the river delta country, especially when using "misleading maps".

From one until five that afternoon, they followed the inland canal until reaching its ultimate eastern outlet. By then, the foul weather had improved, and the sea was not as rough.

With these improved conditions, Father Robaut decided to paddle his kayak the rest of the way to St. Michael on his own. He bid Jack, Charley, and John farewell, then paddled away.

After leaving Jack's company, Father Robaut disappeared. The irony of Roubaut's earlier admission that he had often lost his way was not overlooked by Jack. London commented in his notebook regarding the missing missionary: ". . . never heard of again — lost in some back slough most likely".[48]

For reasons that have never been explained, Jack and his companions spent that night and all the next day camped at the mouth of the inland canal.

The next day, which was Thursday, June 30, the three men got up early. After breaking camp and loading the boat, they sailed straight through to St. Michael. Jack described their arrival:

> Our last taste of the Bering Sea was a fitting close to the trip. Midnight found us wallowing in the sea, a rocky coast to leeward and a dirty sky to windward, with sputters of rain and wind squalls which soon developed into a gale. Removing the sprit and bagging the after-leech, we shortened to storm canvas and ran before it, reaching the harbor of St. Michael just 21 days from the time we cast off the lines at Dawson.[49]

St. Michael was a small port city on the shore of the great Norton Sound which opens to the Bering Sea. It was built in the midst of expansive mud flats. Its buildings were surrounded by an odd assortment of tents, shacks, and shanties. From the wharves at the waterline to its center, nondescript grey warehouses lined the town's long, mud streets. Rusty old Russian cannons could be seen corroding in the abandoned blockhouses, and the smell of dead fish was pervasive.[50]

From the moment Jack and his friends arrived, there was flurry of confusion about what day or date it actually was. The confusion continues to this day. Jack wrote and underlined in his diary, "Find it to be Wednesday 28." But, Wednesday in the last week of June 1898 was the 29th![51]

The final entry in Jack's Yukon River diary reads: "Leave St. Michaels [*sic*] — unregrettable moment".

The next legs of Jack's long journey home would be completed by steamships and, according to some experts, by train. According to Charmian, "Jack stoked his steamship passage from St. Michaels [*sic*] to British Columbia, thence proceeded steerage to Seattle . . . with a few of the twinges of scurvy still within him to remind him of the unlucrative year".[52]

According to Casswell Prewitt, in addition to his place on the rowboat, he had also given Jack a ticket which was good for passage on the passenger ship SS *Bartlett*, sailing from St. Michael to Seattle.

Still other authorities contend that Jack rode the railroads south from Seattle to Oakland. Propounding this theory, Irving Stone wrote, "From Seattle it was an easy matter for a blowed-in-the-glass tramp to beat his way down to Oakland on the freights".[53]

London stated in his account of the voyage, ". . . I had passed coal on a steamship from Bering Sea to British Columbia, and traveled in the steerage from there to San Francisco . . ."[54]

So, just how did Jack get to San Francisco?

Franklin Walker gave us the most probable and lucid scenario with this version: "Ever quick to seize an opportunity, London had obtained a job passing coal on a steamer pushing south to warmer waters. Somewhere between St. Michael and Victoria, he burned himself so badly that he had to give up the job. Perhaps his scurvy crippled or weakened him enough to cause the accident. Or perhaps the explanation is found in a passage in John

Barleycorn. 'I remember passing coal on an ocean steamer through eight days of hell during which time we coal-passers were kept to the job by being fed whisky. We toiled half drunk all the time. And without the whisky we could not have passed the coal.' Such conditions might easily have led to a serious burn. He travelled steerage from British Columbia to San Francisco, arriving home early in August".[55]

If the confusion over what day Jack reached St. Michael is irritating, and the different versions regarding just how London returned to San Francisco are perturbing, then the complete lack of a date for his arrival in San Francisco is absolutely maddening. Not one authority gives an exact date, and Jack never gave us an exact date himself. Charmian London simply says that his time in the Klondike had been an "unlucrative year" and leaves it at that without giving a date. Neither Irving Stone nor Joan London give any date.

The closest approximations are given in terms of the month he arrived. Franklin Walker believed that it was August. Russ Kingman stated that Jack came home from the Klondike in July of 1898. Earle Labor, Milo Shepard, and Robert Leitz have it as *both* early *and* late July in The Letters of Jack London.

The fact is, normally it would have taken about two weeks to travel from St. Michael to San Francisco by passenger steamship. If we accept Jack's version of how he returned, he would have arrived home around July 14, 1898, approximately one year after the day he had left for the Klondike.

Jack London returned home virtually penniless except for a moosehide sack containing a quarter ounce of gold dust extracted from his claim on Henderson Creek. He had not struck it rich as he had hoped. Yet, the unforgettable memories and impressions of his Klondike adventure — the people he had met and the places he had visited — would prove to be worth far more than gold.

Jack London posing in Klondike garb.
Photos taken by Ninetta Eames for her article
about him in the May 1900 issue of *Overland Monthly*.
The photo on the right was used in the article.

Afterword

As Jack London and his two companions began their journey home on the Yukon River in early June 1898, thousands of newly-arriving gold-seekers were flowing into the Klondike gold country. Yet, by mid-1899, the frenzied gold rush was winding down even though millions of dollars worth of gold still remained in the hills and waterways surrounding Dawson.

Dawson, which had not existed before 1896, was one of the largest, liveliest, and most cosmopolitan cities in the entire Northwest by the fall of 1898. The "San Francisco of the North" had grown from a few hundred prospectors in the fall of 1896 to at least 1,500 inhabitants by the spring of 1897. At the height of the gold rush in 1898, about 30,000 people lived in Dawson; thousands more lived in the surrounding areas. This was a small number compared to the hundreds of thousands of fortune-seekers who set out for the Klondike. The remote location and the rugged nature of the region ensured that many travelers would turn back.

In the Klondike, the demands of the environment eliminated the lazy and incompetent. Those who reached the Klondike and were able to survive a Yukon winter earned the distinction of being dubbed "sourdoughs". This elite group was quickly depleted as the diggings played out and the "big strike" failed to materialize.

The picks, shovels, and gold pans of the veteran sourdoughs moved on to other gold strikes in British Columbia, California, Colorado, Nevada, and other parts of North America throughout the latter 19th and early 20th centuries. Towns, cities, and states were created wherever people rushed to find their elusive fortunes in gold.

Gold mining remained a major industry in the Klondike region for the next fifty years. Most of the remaining gold was recovered by big mining companies using huge dredging machines which sifted through tons of gravel each day, accomplishing the work of several hundred sourdoughs. In fact, placer mining is *still* going strong in the Klondike today.

Because of its proximity to the Arctic Circle and its distance from civilization, Dawson imported nearly everything its citizens needed . . . except gold. Within a few years of being settled, Dawson had a telephone service, running water, steam heat, electricity, dozens of hotels, motion-picture theaters, restaurants, dramatic societies, hospitals, physicians, lawyers, and people — from virtually all walks of life and every corner of the world.

The need for a more localized government was soon recognized by the Canadian Parliament and, in 1898, the Yukon Territory was officially carved out of the vast Northwest Territories. Dawson was chosen as the territorial capital and remained so until the 1950s when the capital was moved to Whitehorse, a more populated and accessible town several hundred miles to the south.

Although there have been several gold rushes in North America, none were as dramatic as the great Klondike Gold Rush. As Pierre Berton succinctly wrote: "The Klondike stampede did not start slowly and build up to a climax, as did so many earlier gold rushes. It started instantly with the arrival of the *Excelsior* and *Portland*, reached a fever pitch at once, and remained at fever pitch until the following spring, when, with the coming of the Spanish-American War, the fever died almost as swiftly as it arose. If the war had not come, the rush might have continued unabated for at least another half-year, but, even so, the stampede remains unique. It was the last and most frenzied of the great international gold rushes. Other stampedes involved more gold and more men, but there had been nothing like it before, there has been nothing like it since . . ."[1]

And, its legacy continues to this day.

Jack London's Klondike adventure proved to be a major turning point in his life. From the time of his birth in 1876 to his return from the Klondike in 1898, his experiences, both his successes and failures, provided a type of personal wealth that money cannot buy . . . a rich foundation for his future success as a writer and storyteller.

Shortly after his return from the Klondike, London learned that his stepfather, John London, had died in his absence. His keen sense of duty contributed to his decision to undertake the responsibility of financially supporting his widowed mother, Flora, and his nephew, Johnny Miller. But, Jack London also found the job market and overall economy in a general slump, just as it had been when he had left for the Klondike.

Despite the odds and with renewed determination, Jack vowed to make another effort to succeed as a writer.

Initially, London wrote many pieces but sold nothing. In fact, the number of articles and stories written on the Klondike Gold Rush was overwhelming; many Klondikers who had returned to the States were inundating editors with articles about their experiences and the gold rush. These greenhorn writers felt that what they wrote was desirable and printable, and they were willing to sell their articles for virtually anything they could get.

So, for the first several months after returning from the Northland, Jack lived entirely on money from odd jobs he could hustle. He would write until he was unbearably broke, find a job, earn some money, and then return to his writing until he was once again broke. Jack and his mother made a solemn pact to continue this pattern until they were undeniably beaten or until Jack succeeded in selling his work.

Eventually, his herculean efforts and determination bore fruit, and his work began to sell. A little over one year after his penniless return from the Klondike, London's first book, The Son of the Wolf, was sold to Houghton, Mifflin & Co. It was a collection of stories set in the land of the great gold rush from which he had recently returned.

When it was published in the spring of 1900, the book was a solid success. It is true that the public's interest in the Northland contributed to its popularity, but what really made the book sell was the eloquence and vitality of Jack's writing. His characters were infused with a believable life which he projected against the backdrop of a gargantuan geography, challenged by the utmost extremes of nature, and motivated with the lure of gold. His characters were based on himself and people he had known in the Klondike, and the public enjoyed reading of their trials and adventures.

London's success as a writer was an extremely unusual

accomplishment because traditionally American authors had not come from the ranks of the working class. However, many turn-of-the-century American readers were bored with the aloofness of Victorian literature. They were fed up with the fawning patronization of the publishing establishment and wanted more realistic plots and characters. The gritty perspective of a working-class observer, with a flavor more American than English, was exactly what these readers were craving. The reading public yearned for real life adventures to relieve them of the pressures and insecurities of the modern age brought on by the Industrial Revolution. Jack London's work appeared on the literary scene at exactly the right moment to spearhead a change.

More than that, his work was nothing short of brilliant. One highly respected San Francisco literary critic remarked that he would rather have written "The White Silence" than anything else that had appeared in fiction during the previous ten years.[2] Many other critics were equally impressed. But most importantly, the public was clamoring for more and would buy anything that Jack London wrote.

With his literary and subsequent financial success, at last Jack had broken the grip of poverty that had held him at the bottom of society's ladder for the first twenty-four years of his life. But, Jack did not rest on this impressive achievement. He demanded of himself a thousand words of fresh composition daily. He wrote short stories, articles, essays, books, novels, as well as thousands of business and personal letters.

In 1902, Jack composed what would become his most famous novel, The Call of the Wild. By the time it was published in 1903, more than $100 million in gold dust and nuggets had been gleaned from the Yukon and its tributaries. One hundred years later, that gold has disappeared into the world economy, but The Call of the Wild has become an international favorite, published in more than eighty languages in seemingly countless editions.

London later wrote that, "I brought nothing back from the Klondike but my scurvy".[3] It is true that he returned from the Northland without much more than the clothes on his back, a few grams of gold, and scurvy, but he also came home with something more elusive and invaluable: he had matured and refined his perspective. In an article about himself written years later, Jack related:

> ". . . I left the laundry and wrote all the time, and lived and dreamed again. After three month's trial I gave up writing, having decided that I was a failure, and left for the Klondike to prospect for gold. At the end of the year, owing to an outbreak of scurvy, I was compelled to come out, and on a homeward journey of 1,900 miles in an open boat, made the only notes of the trip. It was in the Klondike I found myself. There nobody talks. Everybody thinks. You get your true perspective. I got mine".[4]

Jack London had developed not only his perspective but also a tremendous strength of personality and intellect with which most other writers could not hope to compete. He had perfected an effective style of communication both in speaking and in writing, and he had grown far beyond what could be expected from a typical 22-year-old man of his time. In spite of a life marked from birth by poverty, hardship, despair, failure, and the inherent struggle for survival at the bottom of society, he had consistently strengthened and improved himself, confidently changing what would have been his natural destiny by sheer force of will. He obtained a unique and impressive education, both in formal schooling and through his own reading and life experiences. He believed in social ideals and intensely desired to find life to be "worth the candle". In general, London saw past the brunt of illusions which would limit the majority of his contemporaries.

As London discovered throughout his life, but especially in the Klondike, he was a natural storyteller who possessed the innate skill of being able to express his ideas with a crisp clarity that incited a reader's (or listener's) imagination. He understood as well as experienced and was able to share that understanding in the way he wrote, spoke, and lived. However, Jack's year in the Klondike had been only one of his numerous adventures; he had been many places, done many things, and met many people. His descriptions of places he had lived and things he had seen allowed readers to feel as though they had also been there. This was especially true for those who wished they had traveled to the

Klondike and wanted to know more about what it was like.

Recently, we celebrated the centennial of the Klondike Gold Rush. During the past 100 years, more than 100 Klondike-related books have been published. London's Northland stories and tales, written nearly a century ago, have not only survived but are virtually the most famous literary works of and about that period.

London came to the Klondike with a burning passion for adventure, a scholar's unquenchable thirst for knowledge, and the body of an athlete. He had "let career go hang, and was on the adventure-path again in quest of fortune".[5] Yet, Jack's year in the Northland had a most important effect — the expansion of his already developed perspective, and not just in the physical sense. London had gained experience, insight, and knowledge on his journey to the Klondike. The essentials of man and nature observed by London on that journey would enhance his work for the rest of his life and enrich world literature forever.

The powerful realism Jack brought to his writing was drawn from the life he had mastered. As an underprivileged, working-class lad with a craving for adventure, Jack discovered a type of triumph independent of money and based upon character and experience. He transformed his adventures into assets by incorporating them into his life and his writing. His life became the epitome of the American dream for future generations of writers, learning by his example that with health, hard work, and determination, we can achieve our dreams, and by doing so, inspire others.

Before he left for the Klondike, neither Jack London nor his friends had any idea that he would return from the Klondike to eventually become one of the true revolutionaries of world literature. London had learned how to tap into the magic and mystery, bringing words to life with a new realism that excited readers worldwide. He became the best-selling, most widely-read, and popular American writer of all time.

Notes

Foreword

The quote at the beginning of the Foreword is by Lowell Thomas Jr., from the Introduction to The Trail of '98, An Anthology of the Klondike, published in 1962.

1. The Yukon took its name from the Indian word, "*diuke-on*", meaning "clear water". The Yukon River runs across the northwesternmost corner of Canada and served as a major "highway" for gold-seekers during the Klondike Gold Rush. In 1898, the newly-established Territory which encompassed the river officially took its name.
2. Jack London and His Times, page 141.
3. Jack London & The Klondike, page 45.
4. Chilkoot Pass, Then and Now, pages 5 and 7.
5. Also known as "El Dorado", a Spanish word for a legendary land of fabulous wealth.
6. Jack London & The Klondike, page 45.
7. Chilkoot Pass, Then and Now, page 20.
8. Jack London and His Times, page 139.
9. The Book of Jack London, page 225.

Over The Chilkoot Pass

Thousands of fortune seekers invaded the Yukon Territory during the Klondike Gold Rush of 1897-1898. Greenhorn gold-seekers were referred to as *Cheechakos* (CHE-cha-kos), from the Chinook word for "new to come". *Cheechakos* were frequently directed to prospect in the hills by unscrupulous Sourdoughs who knew that gold nuggets tended to settle in the river and creek beds. Those who survived a harsh Klondike winter, many of them seasoned veterans from the 1849 California Gold Rush, were referred to as "Sourdoughs", named after the staple bread of the frontier. One cynical Sourdough is quoted as saying, "We were SOUR on the Yukon and didn't have enough DOUGH to get out".

1. John Barleycorn, Chapter XXV.

2. A Pictorial Life of Jack London of Jack London, page 70. According to Satterfield (page 66), the "foolish" old bard described the Klondike as little more than an elegant wilderness hike. The Mounties in Dawson City asked him to leave town because his numerous stories in newspaper and magazines were "misleading tenderfeet into believing the North was something like a park in downtown Cleveland. . . . The poor, silly old man simply could not believe what he saw around him, and convinced himself he was seeing an epic performed before his eyes where everyone was happy and nobody got hurt".

3. Jack London & The Klondike, pages 47-48.

4. Chilkoot Pass, Then and Now, page 108. According to Berton (page 165), no one could enter the Yukon Territory without a year's supply of food, which was about 1,150 pounds, plus everything needed to survive a year in the harsh northern climate "without outside aid".

5. The Book of Jack London, page 224.
6. Jack London & The Klondike, page 48.
7. The Book of Jack London, page 225.
8. Martin Eden, Chapter 27.
9. A Pictorial Life of Jack London, page 71.
10. Jack London & The Klondike, page 49.
11. The Book of Jack London, page 225.
12. Jack London/A Definitive Chronology, page 14.
13. A Daughter of the Snows, page 7.
14. Chilkoot Pass, Then and Now, page 1.
15. The Book of Jack London, page 227.
16. *Ibid.*
17. The Letters of Jack London, Volume I, page 11.
18. Chilkoot Pass, Then and Now, page 182.
19. Jack London & The Klondike, page 56.
20. A Pictorial Life of Jack London, page 71.
21. The Book of Jack London, page 227.
22. Jack London & The Klondike, page 56.
23. Jack, A Biography of Jack London, page 43.
24. Jack London/A Definitive Chronology, page 14.
25. The Book of Jack London, page 228.
26. The Book of Jack London, page 227.

27. According to oral interviews with Martin W. Tarwater's grandson, Francis Tarwater, in December 1996, and his granddaughter, Marion "Caroll" Bessire, in September 1997, their grandfather was born in Missouri and had nine children.

Martin died after a two-month sickness and was buried in Fort Yukon, Alaska, on May 20, 1898. According to Caroll and Francis, a one-room schoolhouse, Tarwater School, near Mark West Springs Road in Santa Rosa, and Tarwater School District [which was in existence until the early 1940s], were named after their grandfather "Mart", who was a much beloved veteran mail carrier ("few men were better known" stated an article in the July 23, 1898 *Press Democrat*) and was well-known for his knowledge about early Sonoma County history.

28. Jack London & The Klondike, page 65.
29. Jack London/A Definitive Chronology, page 14.
30. A Pictorial Life of Jack London, page 72.
31. The Book of Jack London, page 229.
32. Jack London/A Definitive Chronology, page 14.
33. The Book of Jack London, page 228.
34. A Pictorial Life of Jack London, page 72; Jack London/A Definitive Chronology, page 14; Jack London & The Klondike, page 67.
35. Jack London/A Definitive Chronology, page 15.
36. Jack London & The Klondike, page 68.
37. The Book of Jack London, page 228.
38. Jack London & The Klondike, page 71.
39. *Ibid.*
40. Smoke Bellew, Chapter I, "The Taste of Meat".

Life and Death in the Klondike

1. Scotty Allan, the famous Alaskan dogsled driver, quoted in Jack London and His Times, page 143.
2. Jack London: Sailor on Horseback, page 87.
3. A Daughter of the Snows, Chapter XVIII.
4. From "Like Argus of the Ancient Times", included in Jack London's posthumously published, The Red One. The Macmillan Co., New York, 1918.
5. Jack London and His Times, page 143. Today, the name "Yukon" has been generally adopted for this section of river which was known as "the Lewes" when London was in the Klondike.
6. Jack London & The Klondike, page 76.
7. Jack London/A Definitive Chronology, page 15.
8. Jack London/A Definitive Chronology, page 16.
9. Jack London & The Klondike, page 78; Jack London/A Definitive Chronology, page 16.

10. Jack London/A Definitive Chronology, page 16.
11. *Ibid.*
12. Smoke Bellew, Chapter II, "The Meat".
13. The Book of Jack London, page 231. It should be noted that Charmian's version is in error in that Caribou Crossing (known today by the shortened name of Carcross) joins Lakes Bennett and Tagish which in turn connects to Lake Marsh, the next lake downstream to join with the Yukon.
14. From "The Trail of Ninety-Eight", a poem by Robert Service.
15. Chilkoot Pass, Then and Now, page 81.
16. Jack London & The Klondike, page 83.
17. "Through the Rapids on the Way to the Klondike".
18. Smoke Bellew, Chapter II, "The Meat".
19. Tales of Adventure, pages 40-41.
20. Jack London & The Klondike, page 87.
21. A Pictorial Life of Jack London, page 76.
22. "Through the Rapids on the Way to the Klondike".
23. Franklin Walker in Jack London & The Klondike, page 78.
24. Jack London & The Klondike, page 92.
25. From "Like Argus of the Ancient Times".
26. A Pictorial Life of Jack London, page 76.
27. As described in Thompson's diary.
28. Both quotes in this paragraph — and all the short quotes interspersed throughout the next several paragraphs — are excerpts from Thompson's diary.
29. Jack London & The Klondike, page 97; Encyclopedia Britannica, pages 803-805 and 818.
30. Jack London & The Klondike, pages 95-96.
31. It may be assumed that the *Belle of the Yukon* sailed with them or, at the least, was within a few miles. But, this is not known for certain as no reliable record exists to establish this as a fact.
32. Jack London & The Klondike, pages 97-98.
23. Jack London & The Klondike, page 98.
34. Much of the above facts gleaned from Jack London/A Definitive Chronology, page 17, and Jack London & The Klondike, page 99.
35. *National Geographic*, July 1930.
36. Jack London & The Klondike, page 99.
37. Jack London & The Klondike, page 100.
38. A Pictorial Life of Jack London, page 77.

39. The Book of Jack London, page 233.

40. Information for the last three paragraphs from Jack London/A Definitive Chronology, page 17.

41. The last entry in Fred Thompson's diary is dated October 18, 1897. Jack London & The Klondike, page 106.

42. Jack London & The Klondike, page 106.

43. Jack London & The Klondike, page 122.

44. Jack London & The Klondike, page 107.

45. Jack London & The Klondike, page 106.

46. A Pictorial Life of Jack London, page 77.

47. Jack London & The Klondike, pages 111-112.

48. Jack London & The Klondike, page 119.

49. In fairness, it should be mentioned that Jack did address this problem in his future, nonfiction, Socialist writings such as The People of the Abyss.

50. Jack London & The Klondike, page 114.

51. Jack London & The Klondike, page 111.

52. A Daughter of the Snows, Chapter XI.

53. Burning Daylight, Chapter XIII.

54. A Pictorial Life of Jack London, page 77.

55. Jack London & The Klondike, page 10.

56. Jack London & The Klondike, page 109.

57. From "Housekeeping in the Klondike".

58. The Book of Jack London, page 235.

59. The Book of Jack London, page 238.

60. From "Housekeeping in the Klondike".

61. Jack London & The Klondike, page 134. This was undoubtedly a wise option in the years before consumer safety laws, when "rot-gut" whiskey was common and poisonous concoctions were often the cause of compounded tragedy.

62. Jack London & The Klondike, pages 133-134.

63. Miller in a letter dated December 17, 1897, as quoted in Harr Wagner's 1929 book, Joaquin Miller and His Other Self, page 129.

64. Quoted in Jack London: Sailor on Horseback, pages 88-89.

65. This was an excellent idea since the town was prone to fires.

66. Jack London: Sailor on Horseback, page 86. Undoubtedly quoted from Emil Jensen's unpublished manuscript, "Jack London at Stewart River".

67. The Book of Jack London, page 237.

68. Jack London & The Klondike, page 142, and The Book

of Jack London, page 239.

69. Jack London: Sailor on Horseback, page 86.

70. The Book of Jack London, page 240.

71. The Book of Jack London, page 239.

NOTE: This was not the last time Jack London saw Ira "Merritt" Sloper. Sloper (1855-1942) left the Klondike during the same summer as Jack London [1898], according to Jack's May 5, 1900 letter to Cornelius Gepfert. Upon Sloper's arrival in San Francisco, his wife Kate initiated divorce proceedings because he "had not struck it rich" [London's letter to Mabel Applegarth, December 22, 1898]. Before he left for the Klondike, Merritt deeded more than $4,000 in property to his wife. Jack served as a witness, appearing on Sloper's behalf, in the divorce proceedings.

72. Jack London & The Klondike, page 140.

73. Both quotes by Hargrave from The Book of Jack London, page 238.

74. Most authorities agree that the writing is authentic. It certainly looks like Jack's handwriting. That it has lasted for so many years is amazing, though not impossible. In 1969, four years after its rediscovery, the cabin was reconstructed into two cabins using its original logs. One of the cabins was moved to Dawson as an attraction at the Jack London Center there. The other was brought to Jack London Square in Oakland, California, and reassembled near Heinold's First and Last Chance Saloon as a permanent display. See Jack London's Cabin, page 31.

75. Jack London/A Definitive Chronology, page 18.

76. A Pictorial Life of Jack London, pages 78 and 80, and Jack London/A Definitive Chronology, page 18.

77. Jack London & The Klondike, page 147.

78. From "Housekeeping in the Klondike".

79. Letter to Con Gepfert, September 20, 1901 [at the Bancroft Library].

80. Jack London & The Klondike, page 143. [Note: The quotes in this section regarding Stevens and his "Missus" are from pages 143-146.]

81. Jack London & The Klondike, page 145.

82. From Jensen's unpublished manuscript, "Jack London at Stewart River".

83. The Book of Jack London, pages 234-236.

84. The Book of Jack London, page 240.

85. Jack London & The Klondike, page 142.

86. Jack London & The Klondike, page 147. [Original Source: "The Husky", June 30, 1900, *Harper's Weekly*.]

87. Jack London & The Klondike, page 148.

88. This is an important story to remember when stories of Jack London's drunken antics are offered. Despite his undeserved reputation as a drunkard, London was not even remotely an alcoholic. A practicing alcoholic would find it very difficult to save a bottle of whiskey and not open it for months.

89. Jack London & The Klondike, page 140.

80. The Book of Jack London, page 234.

81. Jack London & The Klondike, page 117.

The Long Journey Home

1. A Daughter of the Snows, Chapter 23.
2. A Daughter of the Snows, Chapter 24.
3. Jack London & The Klondike, page 178.
4. The Book of Jack London, page 243.
5. Jack London & The Klondike, page 162.
6. Jack London & The Klondike, pages 166-167. *See also* The Klondike Fever, page 172.
7. The Book of Jack London, page 243.
8. "From Dawson to the Sea".
9. Jack London/A Definitive Chronology, page 18.
10. All uncited quotes from this point in the text to the end of the chapter are taken from Charmian's transcription of Jack's penciled Yukon River diary in The Book of Jack London, Volume I, pages 248-257.
11. "From Dawson to the Sea".
12. Jack London & The Klondike, pages 161-162.
13. "From Dawson to the Sea".
14. Jack London & The Klondike, page 167.
15. "From Dawson to the Sea".
16. *Ibid.*
17. *National Geographic*, July 1930.
18. Jack London/A Definitive Chronology, page 18.
19. Jack London & The Klondike, page 171, and "From Dawson to the Sea".
20. "From Dawson to the Sea".
21. Jack London & The Klondike, page 169.
22. *National Geographic*, July 1930.
23. Jack London & The Klondike, page 178-179.
24. "From Dawson to the Sea".

25. Jack London & The Klondike, page 174.
26. "From Dawson to the Sea".
27. *Ibid.*
28. *Ibid.*
29. Remember that it took Jack and Thompson five days to hike the eighty miles of river trail between Dawson and Split-Up Island, and that was without any additional burden other than what they required for themselves.
30. "From Dawson to the Sea".
31. The Book of Jack London, page 243: ". . . who had sorely suffered with scurvy from the many months lack of fresh meat".
32. "From Dawson to the Sea".
33. Theodore Durrant, "the demon in the belfry", was executed at San Quentin Prison in Marin County, California, on January 7, 1898, for the sensational murders of two young women in a San Francisco church where he had served as the assistant Sunday school superintendent.
34. "From Dawson to the Sea".
35. "That period" was not defined in London's notes and never subsequently revealed.
36. "From Dawson to the Sea".
37. *Ibid.*
38. *Ibid.*
39. *National Geographic*, July 1930.
40. "From Dawson to the Sea".
41. Quoted from "The Law of the Yukon", a poem by Robert Service.
42. "From Dawson to the Sea".
43. *National Geographic*, July 1930.
44. At first, it might seem like these white men had taken advantage of the Indian. In fact, the trade was quite fair. The natives did not raise bread grains or make their own flour, so milled flour was highly prized. And, the salmon were making their run by then, so they were readily available and abundant.
45. The place Bill Moore built retained his name and remains in use to this day.
46. "From Dawson to the Sea".
47. *Ibid.*
48. In fact, Father Robaut was not lost. He continued to live in Alaska until his death on December 18, 1930. He was buried at Holy Cross ("S. Crucis") Mission, which the Jesuit Father had established in the small Russian fishing village of Kozyrevsky (known today as Holy Cross), Alaska.

Father Robaut (pronounced "Roo-bow", thus London's phonetic spelling of "Roubeau"), was born on April 12, 1855. He entered the Jesuit order on March 18, 1883. He arrived in Alaska in 1886. He took his final vows in the Jesuit Order on August 15, 1891. He is recognized for his work with the Innuit language.

49. "From Dawson to the Sea".

50. Jack London & The Klondike, pages 190-191.

51. This author believes that Jack had the correct dates all along, based on a calendar for 1898 which verifies his dates and days of the week.

52. The Book of Jack London, page 257.

53. Jack London: Sailor on Horseback, page 91; Jack London & The Klondike, page 151; Jack London/A Definitive Chronology, page 18.

54. "From Dawson to the Sea".

55. Jack London & The Klondike, page 191. Note: The version advanced by Charmian and Franklin Walker appears to be, most likely, the truth.

Afterword

1. The Klondike Fever, page 100.

2. "The White Silence" is one of the short stories included in Jack London's first book, The Son of the Wolf, which was published in 1900.

3. John Barleycorn, Chapter XXV.

4. "Jack London By Himself", both a pamphlet and published in "Mainly About People".

5. John Barleycorn, Chapter XXV.

Please note that Jack London's
original spelling has been retained
in all direct quotes in this book.

All book titles are underlined,
magazine titles and ship names are italicized,
and titles of newspaper articles, plays,
and pamphlets are in quotations
with the exception of the section entitled
"Jack London's Writings About the Klondike"
in which book titles are italicized and the titles of
short stories, articles, and plays are in quotations.

1897 Calendar

JAN

S	M	T	W	T	F	S
					1	2
3	4	5	6	7	8	9
10	11	12	13	14	15	16
17	18	19	20	21	22	23
24	25	26	27	28	29	30
31						

FEB

S	M	T	W	T	F	S
	1	2	3	4	5	6
7	8	9	10	11	12	13
14	15	16	17	18	19	20
21	22	23	24	25	26	27
28						

MAR

S	M	T	W	T	F	S
	1	2	3	4	5	6
7	8	9	10	11	12	13
14	15	16	17	18	19	20
21	22	23	24	25	26	27
28	29	30	31			

APR

S	M	T	W	T	F	S
				1	2	3
4	5	6	7	8	9	10
11	12	13	14	15	16	17
18	19	20	21	22	23	24
25	26	27	28	29	30	

MAY

S	M	T	W	T	F	S
						1
2	3	4	5	6	7	8
9	10	11	12	13	14	15
16	17	18	19	20	21	22
23	24	25	26	27	28	29
30	31					

JUNE

S	M	T	W	T	F	S
		1	2	3	4	5
6	7	8	9	10	11	12
13	14	15	16	17	18	19
20	21	22	23	24	25	26
27	28	29	30			

JULY

S	M	T	W	T	F	S
				1	2	3
4	5	6	7	8	9	10
11	12	13	14	15	16	17
18	19	20	21	22	23	24
25	26	27	28	29	30	31

AUG

S	M	T	W	T	F	S
1	2	3	4	5	6	7
8	9	10	11	12	13	14
15	16	17	18	19	20	21
22	23	24	25	26	27	28
29	30	31				

SEPT

S	M	T	W	T	F	S
			1	2	3	4
5	6	7	8	9	10	11
12	13	14	15	16	17	18
19	20	21	22	23	24	25
26	27	28	29	30		

OCT

S	M	T	W	T	F	S
					1	2
3	4	5	6	7	8	9
10	11	12	13	14	15	16
17	18	19	20	21	22	23
24	25	26	27	28	29	30
31						

NOV

S	M	T	W	T	F	S
	1	2	3	4	5	6
7	8	9	10	11	12	13
14	15	16	17	18	19	20
21	22	23	24	25	26	27
28	29	30				

DEC

S	M	T	W	T	F	S
			1	2	3	4
5	6	7	8	9	10	11
12	13	14	15	16	17	18
19	20	21	22	23	24	25
26	27	28	29	30	31	

1898 Calendar

JAN

S	M	T	W	T	F	S
						1
2	3	4	5	6	7	8
9	10	11	12	13	14	15
16	17	18	19	20	21	22
23	24	25	26	27	28	29
30	31					

FEB

S	M	T	W	T	F	S
		1	2	3	4	5
6	7	8	9	10	11	12
13	14	15	16	17	18	19
20	21	22	23	24	25	26
27	28					

MAR

S	M	T	W	T	F	S
		1	2	3	4	5
6	7	8	9	10	11	12
13	14	15	16	17	18	19
20	21	22	23	24	25	26
27	28	29	30	31		

APR

S	M	T	W	T	F	S
					1	2
3	4	5	6	7	8	9
10	11	12	13	14	15	16
17	18	19	20	21	22	23
24	25	26	27	28	29	30

MAY

S	M	T	W	T	F	S
1	2	3	4	5	6	7
8	9	10	11	12	13	14
15	16	17	18	19	20	21
22	23	24	25	26	27	28
29	30	31				

JUNE

S	M	T	W	T	F	S
			1	2	3	4
5	6	7	8	9	10	11
12	13	14	15	16	17	18
19	20	21	22	23	24	25
26	27	28	29	30		

JULY

S	M	T	W	T	F	S
					1	2
3	4	5	6	7	8	9
10	11	12	13	14	15	16
17	18	19	20	21	22	23
24	25	26	27	28	29	30
31						

AUG

S	M	T	W	T	F	S
	1	2	3	4	5	6
7	8	9	10	11	12	13
14	15	16	17	18	19	20
21	22	23	24	25	26	27
28	29	30	31			

SEPT

S	M	T	W	T	F	S
				1	2	3
4	5	6	7	8	9	10
11	12	13	14	15	16	17
18	19	20	21	22	23	24
25	26	27	28	29	30	

OCT

S	M	T	W	T	F	S
						1
2	3	4	5	6	7	8
9	10	11	12	13	14	15
16	17	18	19	20	21	22
23	24	25	26	27	28	29
30	31					

NOV

S	M	T	W	T	F	S
		1	2	3	4	5
6	7	8	9	10	11	12
13	14	15	16	17	18	19
20	21	22	23	24	25	26
27	28	29	30			

DEC

S	M	T	W	T	F	S
				1	2	3
4	5	6	7	8	9	10
11	12	13	14	15	16	17
18	19	20	21	22	23	24
25	26	27	28	29	30	31

Jack London's Writings About the Klondike

Novels:

A Daughter of the Snows, 1902
The Call of the Wild, 1903
White Fang, 1906
Burning Daylight, 1910
Smoke Bellew, 1912

Play:

"Scorn of Women", 1906

Collections of Short Stories:

The Son of the Wolf, 1900
- "The White Silence"
- "The Son of the Wolf"
- "The Men of Forty-Mile"
- "In a Far Country"
- "To the Man on Trail"
- "The Priestly Prerogative"
- "The Wisdom of the Trail"
- "The Wife of a King"
- "An Odyssey of the North"

The God of His Fathers, 1901
- "The God of His Fathers"
- "The Great Interrogation"
- "Which Make Men Remember"
- "Siwash"
- "The Man with the Gash"
- "Jan, the Unrepentant"
- "Grit of Women"
- "Where the Trail Forks"
- "A Daughter of the Aurora"
- "At the Rainbow's End"
- "The Scorn of Women"

Children of the Frost, 1902
- "In the Forests of the North"
- "The Law of Life"

Children of the Frost, continued
"Nam-Bok the Unveracious"
"The Master of Mystery"
"The Sunlanders"
"The Sickness of Lone Chief"
"Keesh, the Son of Keesh"
"The Death of Ligoun"
"Li Wan, the Fair"
"The League of the Old Men"

The Faith of Men, 1904
"The Relic of the Pliocene"
"A Hyperborean Brew"
"The Faith of Men"
"Too Much Gold"
"The One Thousand Dozen"
"The Marriage of Lit-Lit"
"Bâtard"
"The Story of Jees Uck"

Love of Life, 1907
"Love of Life"
"A Day's Lodging"
"The White Man's Way"
"The Story of Keesh"
"The Unexpected"
"Brown Wolf"
"The Sun Dog's Trail"
"Negore, the Coward"

Lost Face, 1910
"Lost Face"
"Trust"
"To Build a Fire"
"That Spot"
"Flush of Gold"
"The Passing of Marcus O'Brien"
"The Wit of Porportuk"

Other London Works with Klondike references:

Revolution, 1910
"The Shrinkage of the Planet" (article)
"The Gold Hunters of the North" (article)

The Night Born, 1913
"The Night Born" (story)

The Turtles of Tasman, 1916
"Finish" (story)
"The End of the Story" (story)
The Red One, 1918
"Like Argus of the Ancient Times" (story)

Other Klondike Related Writings:

"Through the Rapids on the Way to the Klondike" (article)
(*The Home Magazine*, June 1899)
"From Dawson to the Sea" (article)
(*Illustrated Buffalo Express*, June 4, 1899)
"The Kind of Mazy May" (children's story)
(*Youth's Companion*, November 30, 1899)
"Economics in the Klondike" (article)
(*The Review of Reviews*, January 1900)
"Pluck and Pertinacity" (children's story)
(*Youth's Companion*, January 1900)
"The Husky" (article)
(*Harper's Weekly*, June 30, 1900)
"Housekeeping in the Klondike" (article)
(*Harper's Bazaar*, September 15, 1900)
"Thanksgiving on Slav Creek" (story)
(*Harper's Bazaar*, November 24, 1900)
"Bald Face" (children's story)
(*The News*, December 1900)
"To Build a Fire" (children's story)
(*Youth's Companion*, May 1902)
"The Fuzziness of Hookla Heen" (children's story)
(*Youth's Companion*, July 1902)
"My Best Short Story" (article)
(*The Grand Magazine*, August 1906,
commentary on "The League of the Old Men")
"Up the Slide" (children's story)
(*Youth's Companion*, October 25, 1906)
"Chased by the Trail" (children's story)
(*Youth's Companion*, September 26, 1907)

Works Cited

Berton, Pierre. The Klondike Fever/The Life and Death of the Last Great Gold Rush. New York: Carroll & Graf Publishers, Inc., 1989 (original publication date: 1958).

Burg, Amos. "To-Day on 'The Yukon Trail of 1898'." National Geographic July 1930: 85-126.

"Ice and Ice Formations." The New Encyclopedia Britannica. 1989 ed.

Kingman, Russ. A Pictorial Life of Jack London. New York: Crown Publishers, Inc., 1979.

Kingman, Russ. Jack London/A Definitive Chronology. Glen Ellen: David Rejl, 1992.

Labor, Earle, Robert C. Leitz, III, and I. Milo Shepard, editors. The Letters of Jack London. Volume One: 1896-1905. Stanford: Stanford University Press, 1988.

London, Charmian. The Book of Jack London. Volume I, New York: The Century Co., 1921.

London, Joan. Jack London and His Times. New York: The Book League of America, 1939.

North, Dick. Jack London's Cabin. Yukon Territory: Jack London Series, Volume I, 1986.

Satterfield, Archie. Chilkoot Pass, Then and Now. Anchorage: Alaska Northwest Publishing Company, 1973.

Shepard, Irving, ed. Jack London's Tales of Adventure. Garden City: Doubleday & Company, 1956.

Sinclair, Andrew. Jack: A Biography of Jack London. New York: Pocket Books, 1977.

Stone, Irving. Jack London: Sailor on Horseback. Garden City: Doubleday & Company, Inc., 1978.

Tryck, Keith. "Rafting Down the Yukon." National Geographic December 1975: 830-861.

Walker, Franklin. Jack London & The Klondike/The Genesis of an American Writer. San Marino: The Huntington Library, 1966.

Works by Jack London utilized in the text

Short Stories and Articles:

"From Dawson to the Sea" (published in the *Illustrated Buffalo Express*, June 4, 1899)

"Housekeeping in the Klondike" (published in *Harper's Bazaar*, September 15, 1900)

"Jack London by Himself" (pamphlet)

"Like Argus of Ancient Times" (published in The Red One, 1918, and in *Hearst's Magazine*, March 1917)

"Through the Rapids on the Way to Klondike" (published in *The Home Magazine*, June 1899, and reprinted in Jack London's Tales of Adventure)

Books:

A Daughter of the Snows, first published in 1902
Burning Daylight, first published in 1910
Martin Eden, first published in 1909
Smoke Bellew, first published in 1912
John Barleycorn, first published in 1913

Index

Acknowledgments

This book is the result of a suggestion by my wife, Margie, who realized that as I diligently worked on my comprehensive biography on Jack London, there lurked between the pages a shorter book with a more timely application. Also, I must thank the many audience members and fans of "my" Jack London appearances during the past fourteen years who consistently requested a book written by me and continued to encourage me.

I am greatly indebted to the many biographers and historians who have written and published their work before me, creating a foundation from which reason can give rise to discernment and ultimately a better understanding of the truth.

I would also like to express my thanks to those who especially helped me during my research: Jo-Ann Lessard, of Parks Canada—Yukon District; Fathers Schmitz and Schoenberg for their help regarding Father Robaut; Heather Jones, Yukon Archives Reference Assistant; Patty Bernstein of the Sonoma County Office of Education and Caitlin Woodbury of the Santa Rosa *Press Democrat* for their assistance regarding Martin Tarwater and other details; Dan Verhalle of the Chilkoot Trail National Historic Site, Parks Canada; and Karl Gurcke, Historical Archaeologist, Klondike Gold Rush National Historic Park.

My thanks to Edward J. White, Curtis Reinhardt, and Norman Gaddini who kindly gave of their time in reading this manuscript and indicating where improvements could be made.

Special thanks to Donna Wines for helping to make the initial printing of this book possible.

And, thanks to Margie Wilson, who served as my editor and research assistant.

Photo Acknowledgments

For their gracious permission to use the documents and photographs in this book, my thanks to: The Yukon Archives — Government Records Collection for the documents on pages 61 and 62; Winifred Kingman of the Jack London Research Center in Glen Ellen for the photographs on pages vi, 6, 76, and 128; and Margie Wilson for the photos of me on the "About the Author" page and back cover.

About the Author

Mike Wilson was born in North Carolina but moved often as a child, having to change schools at least once a year until he was about nine. About that time, a librarian recognized Mike's innate love of books despite his below average reading ability. Under her kind tutelage, he quickly improved his reading skills. By the time Mike was in high school, he had discovered the works of the great American writer, Jack London. Inspired by the earthy eloquence of London's prose in *Martin Eden*, he dreamt of someday becoming an author.

Now, nearly forty years later, Mike is acknowledged as a writer and historian. His articles have been published in numerous magazines and newspapers. The songs he wrote during his sixteen-year career as a performing songwriter have been recorded, published, and have entertained hundreds of audiences.

By 1987, because of his extensive studies, Mike was recognized as an emerging expert on Jack London and was asked to impersonate London for a living history event in Santa Rosa, California. The one-day appearance evolved into a professional portrayal. His depiction of London is a sensitive, in-depth portrayal which strives to faithfully and accurately reveal London's true character. Mike's "Jack" continues to receive critical acclaim and to foster a greater public appreciation of London's tremendous contribution to the world of literature.

Mike constantly expands his knowledge of London's life and work through reading and research. He is currently putting the finishing touches on his latest endeavor — a unique and comprehensive biography about Jack London — which is scheduled to be published in the near future.

With his wife, Margie, their youngest son, and a menagerie of animals, he resides in western Sonoma County, California.

How to Contact the Author

If you wish to contact Mike Wilson or to order addtional copies of this book, write the publisher at:

**WORDSWORTH™
P. O. Box 7132
Santa Rosa, CA 95407 U.S.A.**

Also available from WORDSWORTH™

- **The Wit and Wisdom of Jack London**

  Get to know the fascinating man behind the legend. Read Jack's thoughts and ideas in his own words. This collection of quotations from his writing and letters is more insightful than an autobiography and offers a direct glimpse into his life, mind, and spirit.
- **Jack London Coloring & Activity Book**

  A 40-page book including an overview of Jack London's life, and a variety of activities including opportunities to color, challenging educational activities such as word search, word games, and more!
- **Jack London Commemorative Bookmark Set**

  A collector's set of four full-color bookmarks, each illustrating and describing an important period in Jack London's life. Learn about Jack as a sailor, rancher and farmer, writer, and his adventures in the Klondike. Educational and practical!
- **"500 Ways to Say Said"**

  The answer to every writer's – and teacher's – dreams! Over 500 different action verbs for use in conversational writing. Improves your writing style instantly!

For more details and information about these and other products, write the address above or visit the WORDSWORTH™ website and its Virtual Bookstore at:

http://www.getyourwordsworth.com

Mike Wilson as Jack London . . .

"The Ultimate Experience with Jack London"

Considered by many to be a "local treasure", Mike Wilson, Sonoma County writer, publisher, and historian, has studied Jack London for nearly two decades. Mike was originally inspired by the earthy eloquence of London's prose when he was a teen-ager. He first portrayed Jack in 1987 for a living history event at the Luther Burbank Home & Gardens in Santa Rosa, California. He was immediately requested by local educators to appear as Jack London for school assemblies and classroom presentations. Widespread word-of-mouth recommendations contributed to Mike's decision to turn his "hobby" into a professional portrayal. He has since performed throughout Northern California for schoolchildren of all ages, at a wide range of special events and conferences, and has been the featured guest speaker for numerous clubs and business and social organizations, including the prestigious Century Club's Centennial Celebration in San Francisco.

He also conducts personal tours of Jack's beloved Beauty Ranch which is now Jack London State Historic Park in Glen Ellen, California. School groups, organizations, business groups, tourists, and entertainers have enjoyed having "Jack" guide them through the Park for the day.

Because of his acknowledged expertise about London's life, Mike was consulted by Walt Disney Entertainment for its CD on Jack London. Many of his articles about Jack London have been published. Mike is currently putting the finishing touches on a definitive biography about Jack London.

Mike's portrayal reveals much of the true character of this adventurous, vivacious man who is considered by many to be the best American author of this century. It is a sensitive, in-depth portrayal, filled with winsome anecdotes, personal glimpses, and insights into turn-of-the-century America, and has been applauded and appreciated by educators, business groups, and audiences of all ages.

To learn more about his portrayal, visit him on the World Wide Web by clicking on his photo at:

http://www.getyourwordsworth.com

or you may telephone him at: 707-829-2316